# Essential Telephoning in English

**Student's Book**

Barbara Garside
Tony Garside

CAMBRIDGE
UNIVERSITY PRESS

CAMBRIDGE UNIVERSITY PRESS
Cambridge, New York, Melbourne, Madrid, Cape Town, Singapore, São Paulo

Cambridge University Press
The Edinburgh Building, Cambridge CB2 2RU, UK

www.cambridge.org
Information on this title: www.cambridge.org/9780521783880

First published 2002
3rd printing 2005

Printed in Italy by Eurografica (part of the LEGO group)

*A catalogue record for this publication is available from the British Library*

ISBN-13  978-0-521-78388-0  Student's Book
ISBN-10  0-521-78388-7  Student's Book

ISBN-13  978-0-521-78389-7  Teacher's Book
ISBN-10  0-521-78389-5  Teacher's Book

ISBN-13  978-0-521-78391-0  Audio CD
ISBN-10  0-521-78391-7  Audio CD

ISBN-13  978-0-521-78390-3  Audio Cassette
ISBN-10  0-521-78390-9  Audio Cassette

## A note from the authors

Writing *Essential Telephoning in English* has made us realise how many people there are who find telephoning difficult, even in their own language. It is not unusual for people to feel stress when the phone rings, or even panic when they make a call and a machine answers. It is difficult to talk to a machine or to someone whose face you can't see, and it can be hard when someone calls you, and you are not prepared for it.

If you don't feel confident in your own language, you probably feel even less confident in a foreign language, especially one you are still learning. In writing this course we have tried to remember these difficulties, and the material in each unit is designed to give you the skills you need to use the phone effectively and to build your confidence in a systematic way.

We hope you find the course useful and enjoyable and, most importantly, that it achieves its aims of improving your telephoning skills in English – and perhaps even in your own language as well.

# 1 Answering the phone

## Lesson A

- Answering the phone in different ways
- Understanding and saying telephone numbers

> **Imagine that the phone is ringing and you have to answer it. Which of the following can help you? Discuss with a partner.**
>
> - Have a pen and some paper ready.
> - Think about which language the caller will speak.
> - Pick the phone up immediately.
> - Sound friendly and interested.

## Listening 1

1.1 **Listen to eight people answering the phone. Which calls include:**

| | |
|---|---|
| a person's name ?    _2_ | an extension number? |
| a company name ? | two phone numbers? |
| a department name? | |

**Check with a partner.**

## Listening 2

1.1 **Listen again and fill in the gaps.**

1 ............................. .

2 Good morning. Jo Cobb .......................... .

3 ........................... Pizzas.

4 Sorry I'm not here to ................ .......................... ..................... .
........................... me on 01273 56218, or try my .................. :
....... 79....... ....... 81....... ....... 0 ....... ....... .

5 ........................... Roberts.

6 Production ................. . ....... ............ ............ .......................... ?

7 ........................... 3....... ....... 7.

8 ........................... Publishing. Piero Dolce ......................... .

**Check with a partner.**

## Language focus

### Pronunciation: intonation

1.1  **1 Listen again to the people answering the phone. Two of them don't
sound as friendly as the others. Which two?**

The others sounded better because they were friendly and interested.
Think of a single note in music that is repeated. This sounds dull.
Compare with these notes. They sound better because they go up and down.

This is what we mean by 'intonation'. When we speak, we need to make our
voice go up and down so that we sound interested and friendly.

1.2  **2 Listen to more people answering the phone and tick (✓) the ones
whose intonation makes them sound interested and friendly.**

1......  2......  3......  4......  5......  6......  7......  8......  9......  10......

**Check with a partner.**

1.3  **3 Listen to all the good examples you've heard and repeat them. Try to
copy the intonation.**

Use single numbers when saying telephone numbers, and group them with
pauses (e.g. 21-37 = 'two one - three seven', not 'twenty-one thirty-seven').

1.4  **1 Listen to these numbers and mark the pauses.**

**a** 677|622   **b** 5024   **c** 439751   **d** 3811675   **e** 00442083165249

1.5  **2 Listen to these phone numbers and write them down, with spaces
where the speakers pause.**

a ...................................................   b ...................................................   c ...................................................
d ...................................................   e ...................................................

Note that double numbers like 55 can be spoken as 'five-five' or 'double-five'.
0 is usually pronounced 'oh' or 'zero', not 'nought'.

## Practice

**Work in pairs. Take turns to do the following.**

1 Your partner will 'call' you five times. Answer the phone in a different way
each time. Sound friendly and interested in all the calls except one. Then ask
your partner to tell you which answer was unfriendly.

2 Say a simple answering machine message containing a phone number. Your
partner will write down the number. Check that they have written the number
correctly.

## Lesson B

- Understanding and saying company names
- Pronouncing letters

**Which of these ways do/would you use to answer the phone at work?**

- Answer with 'Hello'.
- Answer with your number.
- Answer with your name.
- Answer with the name of your company.
- Answer with the name of your department.
- Use a combination or a different way.

**Which way do you prefer? Why? Discuss with a partner.**

## Listening 1

 1.6

**Listen to six people answering the phone using the name of their company. Tick (✓) the company names you hear.**

| | | | | | |
|---|---|---|---|---|---|
| **1** MBM | ✓ | NVM | | NBM | |
| **2** AEK | | EAK | | EAJ | |
| **3** BGB | | PJB | | PJP | |
| **4** SJI | | FJY | | SJY | |
| **5** DTW | | TDV | | TDW | |
| **6** ARP | | RAP | | ARB | |

## Listening 2

1.7

**Listen to six people answering the phone. Match the two halves of the company names.**

**1** JHA     **a** Engineering
**2** GVR     **b** Transport
**3** NEQ     **c** Communications
**4** BIF     **d** Technology
**5** LDC     **e** Travel
**6** OZ     **f** Electronics

# Language focus

## Pronunciation: letters

Letters and spelling are particularly important on the phone.

**Look at the alphabet below. Why has it been written in this way? Discuss with a partner.**

| /eɪ/ <br> day | /iː/ <br> see | /e/ <br> bed | /aɪ/ <br> my | /əʊ/ <br> no | /uː/ <br> you | /ɑː/ <br> are |
|---|---|---|---|---|---|---|
| Aa <br> Hh <br> Jj <br> Kk | Bb <br> Cc <br> Dd <br> Ee <br> Gg <br> Pp <br> Tt <br> Vv <br> Zz (AmE) | Ff <br> Ll <br> Mm <br> Nn <br> Ss <br> Xx <br> Zz (BrE) | Ii <br> Yy | Oo | Qq <br> Uu <br> Ww | Rr |

1.8  **Listen to the pronunciation of the letters. Were you right? Listen again and practise.**

# Practice

**Work in pairs. Take turns to do the following.**

**1** Look at these company names. Read them out to your partner in any order you like. Say one of them incorrectly (e.g. 'CUB' instead of 'CUP'). Your partner writes down the names in the order they hear them, and puts a cross next to the incorrect one. Check what your partner has written.

**2** Your partner will 'call' you five times. Answer the phone in different ways, but include a company name (e.g. IBM, or your own company's name) each time. Your partner writes down the company names. Check that your partner has written them down correctly.

# Language summary

**See page 74 for a summary of the language you have learnt in this unit.**

# 2 | Beginning a call

## Lesson A

- Introducing yourself
- Asking to speak to someone
- Responding to a caller

**When you make a call and introduce yourself, which of the following should you do? Tick (✓) *always*, *sometimes* or *never*. Discuss with a partner.**

|  | always | sometimes | never |
|---|---|---|---|
| • Give your name. | ............ | ............ | ............ |
| • Give a greeting. | ............ | ............ | ............ |
| • Give your telephone number. | ............ | ............ | ............ |
| • Say why you are calling. | ............ | ............ | ............ |
| • Give your address. | ............ | ............ | ............ |
| • Give the name of your company. | ............ | ............ | ............ |
| • Explain your relationship to the person you are calling. | ............ | ............ | ............ |
| • Give your credit card number. | ............ | ............ | ............ |

## Listening 1

2.1 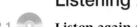 **Listen to the beginning of four conversations. Write down the company names in 1 and 3 and the extension numbers in 2 and 4.**

1 ............................................................................................

2 ............................................................................................

3 *Tara* ...................................................................................

4 ............................................................................................

## Listening 2

2.1 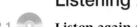 **Listen again and complete the sentences.**

*Introducing yourself*

1 ................................ ................................ David.

2 ................................ Tina ................................ .

3 ................................ ................................ Jana Corte.

4 Miguel ................................ .

"I said: I'm thinking of calling it a TELEPHONE!!!"

*Asking for someone*

1 Is Chris ........................................ ?

2 ........................................ ........................................ speak to Jo, please?

3 I'd ........................................ ........................................ ........................................
Alain, please.

4 ........................................ ........................................ Diane?

## Language focus

**Match the sentences (1–5) to the responses (a–e). There may be more than one possibility.**

*Introducing yourself /*
*Asking to speak to someone*

1 Good morning. It's Franco here.
2 This is Maria. Is that Jack?
3 I'd like to speak to Manju, please.
4 Is Klara in?
5 Could I speak to Peter, please?

*Responding*

a Yes, it is.
b Yes, she is. Just a moment.
c Oh, hello. How are you?
d No, I'm sorry, he's away this week.
e Speaking.

**Now practise with a partner.**

## Practice

1 **Write three conversations using different combinations of the language you have learnt.**

**Example**

A: (answering)           *Good morning. [name of company]*

B: (introducing/asking)  *Hello, this is … . Is … there, please?*

A: (responding)          *Speaking.*

2 **Practise reading the conversations aloud with a partner. Then practise without reading.**

# Lesson B

- Checking who is calling
- Clarifying who you are / why you're calling

**Look at the things you can say when you introduce yourself (1–6). Match them to their functions – the reasons why you say them (a–f).**

1 We worked together in Germany.
2 I work in Marketing.
3 This is Yusuf Kemal.

4 I'm calling about the meeting.
5 Good afternoon.
6 I'm calling from ABC.

a to give your name
b to say why you are calling
c to explain your relationship to the person you are calling
d to give the name of your department
e to give the name of your company
f to greet the other person

## Listening 1

2.2  **Listen to how the four conversations from Lesson A continue. The person answering checks who is calling. Tick (✓) the phrases you hear.**

Sorry, who's speaking, please? .........
Sorry, who's calling, please? .........
I'm sorry, who shall I say is calling? .........
Sorry, who is that? .........
Sorry, what was your name? .........
Sorry, what did you say your name was? .........
And your name is … ? .........
And your name again … ? .........
And you are … ? .........

## Listening 2

2.2  **1 Listen again. The four callers clarify who they are in different ways. Write the number of the conversation in which they:**

say why they are calling .........
mention something that happened recently .........
say where they're from .........
describe their relationship .........

**2 Look at Transcript 2.2 on page 87. Read the conversations with a partner to practise checking who is calling and clarifying who you are.**

## Language focus

There are a number of different ways of clarifying who you are / saying why you are calling at the beginning of a call:

| name ... | *from + company* |
| | *from + office, place* |
| | *I'm his business partner.* |
| | *he's my line manager.* |
| | *we met at ...* |
| | *she rang me ...* |
| | *they worked with us ...* |
| | *I'm calling/phoning/ringing about / to discuss the conference.* |

**In the following sentences, people clarify who they are or say why they're calling. Complete each sentence using one word. There may be more than one possibility.**

1  I'm calling ........................... the meeting.

2  I'm ringing ........................... ask about the next delivery.

3  It's Ana here, ........................... head office.

4  I worked ........................... her last month.

5  He came to a meeting ........................... our office recently.

### Pronunciation: stress

**Look at the sentences above again. Work with a partner and <u>underline</u> the most important words – the words that are stressed. Say the sentences aloud to each other to help you. What kind of words are usually stressed?**

2.3  **Listen and check.**

## Practice

**Do the role plays in Communication activities.**
STUDENT A: turn to page 58.
STUDENT B: turn to page 65.

## Language summary

See page 75 for a summary of the language you have learnt in this unit.

# 3 Ending a call

## Lesson A

- Recognising the end of a conversation
- Signalling the end of a conversation

---

**Read this text and fill in the gaps using these words:**

finish   this   harder   politely   'Goodbye'   call   person

It's easy to end a phone (1)................................. – just say (2)................................. .
It's much (3)................................. to *signal* the end – to show the other
(4)................................. that you want to (5)................................. the call. But there
are several ways of doing (6)................................. clearly and (7)................................. .

## Listening 1

3.1   **Listen to the ending of five conversations and answer the questions.**

1 Who was worried, the man or the woman?
2 Who does the woman send good wishes to?
3 Who will make the next call, the man or the woman?
4 What is the e-mail address?
5 Who went to a conference, the man or the woman?

## Listening 2

3.1   **Listen again and number the phrases used for signalling the end of the
conversation in the order that you hear them.**

| | | | |
|---|---|---|---|
| Glad you were in. | | I must get on. | ....1.. |
| Nice to make contact at last. | ......... | Good to hear about ... | ......... |
| Thank you for phoning. | ......... | Speak to you soon. | ......... |
| Thanks for calling back. | ......... | Give me a ring or send me | ......... |
| Thank you for getting back to me. | ......... | an e-mail. | ......... |
| Give my regards to ... | ......... | | |

**Which of the phrases above shows most clearly that someone wants the
conversation to end?**

## Language focus

Notice the following structures in phrases used to signal the end of a conversation:

*Infinitive (without 'to')*
   *Speak to you soon. / Talk to you next week.*
   (= I'll speak/talk …)

Usually used only with *speak/talk*.

*Adjective + infinitive (with 'to')*
   *Good/Nice/Great to hear about … / to make contact.*
   (= It was good …)

*Imperative*
   *Give me a ring. / Give her my regards.*

*'Thank you' / 'Thanks for' + -ing form*
   *Thanks for calling (me) back / ringing.*

**Work with a partner. For each of the structures, write down two more phrases you could use at the end of a phone conversation.**

## Practice

**Put these lines in the correct order to make conversations. There may be more than one possibility.**

**1**

|        |                                          |
|--------|------------------------------------------|
| ……… | All right. Well, thanks for calling.     |
| ……… | Yes, bye.                                |
| ……… | That's OK. Speak to you soon.            |
| ..1.. | Sorry, but I really must get on now.     |

**2**

|        |                                          |
|--------|------------------------------------------|
| ……… | And give my regards to Bob.              |
| ..1.. | Thank you for ringing.                   |
| ……… | Yes, bye.                                |
| ……… | Of course I will. See you then.          |
| ……… | That's OK. Good to speak to you again.   |

**3**

|        |                                          |
|--------|------------------------------------------|
| ……… | Oh, are you? OK.                         |
| ……… | Right, well, good to hear from you.      |
| ……… | Goodbye.                                 |
| ..1.. | Speak to you next week then.             |
| ……… | Yes, nice to talk to you, too.           |
| ……… | Bye for now.                             |
| ……… | Fine. I'm away on Monday, though.        |

**Now practise the conversations with a partner.**

# Lesson B

• Making offers and requests at the end of a conversation

**Rewrite these phrases, putting the words in the correct order.**

1 getting me back to for thanks
  *Thanks for getting back to me.*
2 regards them then give my
3 back calling you me thank for much very

4 later then you talk to
5 weekend a good have
6 contact last nice make to at

## Listening 1

3.2

**Listen to four conversations. In which conversation is each of the following mentioned? Listen again and write down the details.**

a time          ........  ........................................
a day           ........  ........................................
a telephone number ........  ........................................
a name          ...1...   *Phil Davies*

## Listening 2

3.2

**Listen again and complete the following.**

In Conversation **1**, the woman offers to fax the details.
She says: '........................ fax the details.'

In Conversation **2**, the man asks the woman to call on Tuesday.
He says: 'So,........................ ........................ call on ........................?'

In Conversation **3**, the man offers to ........................ the package at 11 o'clock.
He says: '........................................................ .'

In Conversation **4**, the woman asks the man to ........................
the ........................ part.

She says: 'Sorry,........................................................ .'

*"I'm sorry I ever taught him to speak."*

## Language focus

Notice how *I'll ...* and *Could you ...?* are often used towards the end of conversations when we are making offers and requests:

*I'll fax the details.*
*Could you call on Tuesday?*

## Pronunciation: chunking

**When we speak, we group words according to meaning and pause between these groups of words. This is called 'chunking'. Look at these lines from the conversations in Recording 3.2. Decide where there are pauses and 'chunk' the sentences, as in the first one. Work with a partner and say the lines to each other to help you.**

1  OK,/fine./ Well,/thanks, Mr Davies./ I'll fax the details.
2  So, could you call on Tuesday?
3  All right then. I'll deliver the package at 11 o'clock.
4  Sorry, could you repeat the second part?

3.3  **Now listen and check.**

**Write down phrases you could say in these situations, using *I'll* ... and *Could you ...?***

1  You ask the other person to e-mail the November report to you.
   *Could you e-mail the November report to me?*
2  You offer to e-mail the November report to the other person.

   ................................................................................

3  You offer to call the other person tomorrow afternoon.

   ................................................................................

4  You would like the other person to discuss the problem with her boss.

   ................................................................................

5  You want the other person to phone you back.

   ................................................................................

6  You offer to work late so that you can finish the report.

   ................................................................................

**Check your answers with a partner. Then think of possible responses. Practise the sentences and responses, paying particular attention to chunking.**

## Practice

**Do the role plays in Communication activities.**
   STUDENT A: turn to page 58.
   STUDENT B: turn to page 65.

## Language summary

**See page 76 for a summary of the language you have learnt in this unit.**

## Listening

4.1  **1 Listen and write down the phone numbers and company names you hear.**

a ......................................................................................................................................

b ......................................................................................................................................

c ......................................................................................................................................

d ......................................................................................................................................

**2 Write down two company names and two phone numbers. Take turns
to dictate these to your partner (including spelling out the company
names). Your partner writes them down. Check together at the end.**

## Language focus

**Fill in the gaps in these conversations.**

**1**

A: Good morning. AOK Communications.

B: Hello. ............................... I speak ............................... Pat, please?

A: Certainly. Who ............................... I ............................... is ............................... ?

B: ............................... Franco Baggio. We met at the trade show.

**2**

A: Well, nice to make ............................... at last.

B: Yes, thanks for ............................... back to me.

A: That's OK. ............................... send you an e-mail tomorrow.

B: Thanks. Give my ............................... to Simran.

A: I will. Bye.

B: Goodbye.

**3**

A: Thank you for ............................... me back.

B: That's all right. I'm ............................... you were in.

A: ............................... you fax me the details?

B: Yes, ............................... fax them this afternoon.

A: OK, thanks. ............................... to you soon then.

B: Yes. Bye.

**Practise the conversations with a partner, paying attention to pronunciation.**

# Practice

**1 You are beginning a call. Practise this conversation with a partner. Take turns to play each role.**

**STUDENT A**

Answer the phone with a company name.

Repeat the company name.

Respond; check B's name.

Ask B to wait.

**STUDENT B**

Check the company name.

Introduce yourself and ask for someone.

Clarify who you are.

**2 Now practise a similar conversation in Communication activities.**
   **STUDENT A: turn to page 59.**
   **STUDENT B : turn to page 66.**

# New language

If you think a caller has the wrong number, you can say:

*I think you've got the wrong number.*
*This is 316549.*

The caller can reply:

*Oh, sorry to trouble you.*

If you make a call and think you have the wrong number, you can say:

*I'm sorry. I think I've got the wrong number.*

The person answering can reply:

*Don't worry. / That's OK. / No problem.*

**Now do the role play on pages 59 and 66 again. This time use the language above to help you with any problems. Take turns to play each role.**

---

**See page 77 for a summary of the new language you have learnt in this unit.**

---

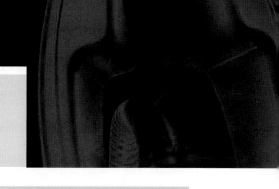

# 5 | Connecting people

## Lesson A

- Asking for a person and a department
- Asking the caller to wait
- Telling the caller they'll be connected

Look at the list of company departments in Listening 1 below.
Discuss with a partner what each department is responsible for.

5.1  ## Listening 1

Listen to four conversations.
Write the number of the
conversation next to the
department mentioned
in it. Two departments
aren't mentioned.

IT ...........
Customer Services ...........
Human Resources ...........
Marketing ...........
Accounts ...........
Sales ...........

5.1  ## Listening 2

Listen again and fill in the gaps in these sentences.

1 ............................................... you through.

2 ............................................... the ............................................... , please.

3 ............................................... I ............................................... someone in IT, please?

4 a ............................................... I ............................................... the Personnel Department?

   b It's ............................................... you.

## Language focus

**1  Put the sentences you completed in Listening 2 under these headings.**

*Asking for a department /person*    *Asking someone to wait*    *Connecting*

..................................................    ..................................................    ..................................................

..................................................    ..................................................    ..................................................

..................................................    ..................................................    ..................................................

..................................................

**2  Here are some more sentences from Recording 5.1. Put them under the headings above.**

Just a moment, please.
Could you put me through to Accounts, please?
Todd can take your call now.
Could you hold, please?
You're through now.
I'd like to speak to Todd in Marketing, please.

5.1  **3  Listen to the conversations again. Then practise them with a partner. (You can use Transcript 5.1 on page 89 to help you.)**

## Practice

**Put these lines in the correct order to make conversations.**

**1**

........  Fine. Who shall I say is calling?
........  Thank you. Hold the line, please ... It's ringing for you ...
........  Oh, good morning. I'd like to speak to Mr Costa in IT, please.
..1..  Key Finance Company. Can I help you?
........  Ann Thompson.

**2**

........  Good afternoon. Could I have someone in Accounts, please?
........  Rob Sparkes. S-P-A-R-K-E-S.
........  Trying to connect you, Mr Sparkes ... Putting you through to Accounts now ...
........  Accounts, yes. And your name is ...?
........  Key Finance Company. How can I help you?

**Now practise the conversations with a partner.**

# Lesson B

- Saying someone is not available
- Responding when someone is not available

**Without looking back at Lesson A, write down the following:**

1 another name for *Personnel Department*
2 a way of asking someone to repeat their name
3 two ways of asking someone to wait
4 three ways of telling someone you will connect them

**Compare your answers with a partner. Then look at Lesson A and Transcript 5.1 on page 89 to check.**

## Listening 1

5.2 **Listen to six conversations. Tick (✓) the ones where the caller gets through to the person/department they want. Put a cross (✗) next to the ones where the caller doesn't get through.**

1 ........ 2 ........ 3 ........ 4 ........ 5 ........ 6 ........

## Listening 2

5.3 **1 Listen again to the four conversations where the caller doesn't get through. Write the number of the conversation(s) in which the person the caller asks for is:**

already on the phone ........ ........
doing something else ........
going to phone the caller back ........

5.3 **2 Listen again. How does the person answering the phone say that someone is:**

*already on the phone*

1 Sorry, ............................ ............................ ............................ at the moment.
2 His line's ............................, I'm afraid.

*doing something else*

3 ............................ ............................ Lynn ............................ ............................ just now.

*going to phone the caller back*

4 ............................ ............................ you ............................ in five minutes.

5.4 **3 Listen to the sentences and practise saying them.**

## Language focus

**Look at the questions (1–3) you can ask after saying someone's not available. Match them to the responses (a–c).**

1  Would you like to hold?
2  Shall I try someone else for you?
3  Could you call back later?

a  Yes, I'll ring back this afternoon.
b  Yes, I will for a couple of minutes.
c  Yes, please. Is Anna there?

### Pronunciation: intonation

1  **Does the intonation rise ➔ or fall ➘ on the questions and responses above? Work with a partner and say them aloud to each other to help you.**

    **Then listen and check.**

2  **Write a sentence to show someone can't answer the phone, followed by a question. Say them to a partner. Your partner replies with a suitable response. Pay particular attention to intonation.**

    **Then work with different partners to see what responses you get this time.**

Example
A:  *Her line's busy at the moment. Would you like to ring later?*
B:  *OK, I'll try again this afternoon.*

## Practice

**Do the role plays in Communication activities.**

> STUDENT A: turn to page 59.
> STUDENT B: turn to page 66.

## Language summary

**See page 78 for a summary of the language you have learnt in this unit.**

*"Would you like to hear some music while you hold?"*

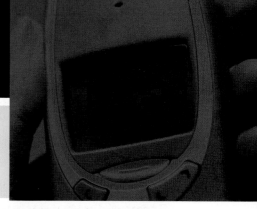

# 6 | Messages 1

## Lesson A

- Answering someone else's phone
- Offering to take a message
- Asking for time to prepare

Who do you take messages for? Write *often, sometimes* or *never*. Discuss with a partner.

|  | In your language | In English |
|---|---|---|
| People at work | ............................ | ............................ |
| People at home | ............................ | ............................ |

## Listening 1

6.1  **Listen to three conversations. In each one, the person the caller wants isn't there. Make a note of where they are.**

1 Clare Aston .........................................
2 Ole Kirsten .........................................
3 Sam Shilton .........................................

## Listening 2

6.1  **Listen again and complete the lines spoken by the people who answer the phone.**

1 Clare ........................ ........................ .
  No, ........................ ........................ she's ........................ ........................ this week.
  Yes. Can I ........................ ........................ ........................ ?
  OK, just a moment ........................ ........................ ........................ ........................ ........................ ...

2 Ole ........................ ........................ .
  No, I'm sorry. He's ........................ ........................ ........................ at the moment.
  ........................ ........................ ........................ a message?
  Just ........................ ........................ a moment then ...

3 Terry and Co. Sam Shilton's ........................ .
  Sorry, ........................ he's ........................ from his ........................ just now.
  ........................ ........................ ........................ message ........................ ........................ ........................ .
  No problem. ........................ ........................ a notepad. ........................ ...

6.1  **Check with a partner and then listen again. Practise the conversations.**

## Language focus

**1  Complete this table with sentences from Listening 2.**

| *Offering to take a message* | *Asking for time to prepare* |
|---|---|
| .................................................. | .................................................. |
| .................................................. | .................................................. |
| .................................................. | .................................................. |

**2  Look at these ways of answering someone else's phone.**

> *Clare Aston's phone/desk/office.*
> *Mo Ward's extension/number.*
> *Extension 321.*

## Practice

**Practise these conversations with a partner. Take turns to play each role.**

**1  STUDENT A**                    **STUDENT B**

Answer Fritz Klein's phone.

Ask to speak to Fritz.

Apologise and say why Fritz isn't
available. Offer to take a message.

Accept the offer.

Ask for time to prepare.

**2  STUDENT A**                    **STUDENT B**

Answer Su Ling's phone.

Introduce yourself and ask to
speak to Su.

Say Su is not available. Check
B's name.

Spell out your name and clarify
who you are.

Offer to take a message.

Say 'No' and that you'll call
again.

# Lesson B

- Taking messages
- Writing a message for someone else

**Think about taking a message in your language or in English. Which of these things do you do to help you? Discuss with a partner.**

- Have a notepad and pen near the phone.
- Ask the caller for time to prepare.
- Ask for repetition when you're not sure.
- Other (what?).

## Listening 1

Look at these messages. Underline the key words (the ones you think are most important). Compare with a partner. The first one is done for you.

**1**

Mike Turner called from the Manchester office. Please e-mail your report to him by Thursday.

**2**
Ms Khan has some questions about the July conference. Phone her as soon as possible.

**3**
Fernando de los Rios of West One Studios rang. He's coming on Tuesday 14th at 2.

**4**
Tricia Smart from EQ Electrics hasn't received the package. Call her on 01242 679824 or e-mail her: t.smart@eqelec.com.

6.2  Listen and check. What do the callers do to show what the key words are? What kind of words are they?

## Listening 2

6.3  Listen to four people leaving messages. The person writing out the messages has made a mistake in three of them. Correct the mistakes where necessary and tick (✓) the correct message.

**1**

Jan

Ms Rivers phoned about last month's delivery. Please fax or e-mail the details to her if you have them.

**2**

Melis

Sara phoned. Could you phone her back next Tuesday?

**3**

Jo

Fax the order to Ken before 12 on Thursday. He will make sure the new machines arrive at the beginning of May.

**4**

Nita

Urgent – phone Jose tomorrow to plan the agenda for next month's meeting.

## Language focus

**Look at the messages in Listening 1. Compare them with what the people actually said (see Transcript 6.2 on page 91).**

### Example

*'Could she e-mail her report to me …?'*
→ *Please e-mail your report to him …*

**Now look at what this person said and write down the message.**

*'This is Paula from Sales. Can she call me as soon as she gets in?'*

> messages

### Pronunciation: stress

6.4

**Listen to what two callers say when they leave a message. Write down the words they stress. Then use the key words to help you write out each message.**

1 .................................................................................................
2 .................................................................................................

## Practice

6.5

**Listen to two conversations where the callers leave a message. Make a note of each message. Then write it out clearly. Swap messages with a partner and compare.**

## Language summary

**See page 79 for a summary of the language you have learnt in this unit.**

# 7 | Messages 2

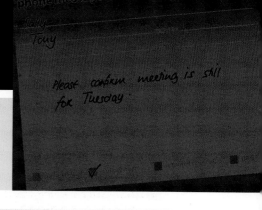

## Lesson A

- Preparing to leave a message
- Leaving a message
- Clarifying details

It is often necessary to leave a message, so it's always a good idea to be ready to do this. How can you prepare to leave a message? Discuss with a partner.

## Listening 1

 7.1

Listen to five conversations where callers leave messages. In which conversation does the message contain:

a request to receive something?          .........
the name of a department?                .........
a place where the caller is going?       .........
a telephone number?                      .........
an offer to finish something?            .........

## Listening 2

7.1

Listen again and note the following.

1 the phone number                ................................................................................

  the person to speak to          ................................................................................

2 what the caller offers to do    ................................................................................

  the name of the company        ................................................................................

3 what the caller wants to receive ................................................................................

  where the warehouse is          ................................................................................

4 where the caller is going       ................................................................................

  the e-mail address              ................................................................................

5 the name of the department      ................................................................................

  the total                       ................................................................................

 7.2

Check by listening to the callers leaving the messages again. This time they clarify the important details (e.g. *16 – that's one six*).

## Language focus

Notice how the speakers in Recording 7.2 clarified difficult words:

*that's* + spelling the name

*... is spelt ...*

using a common word for letters that sound like other letters (e.g. N and M)

**1  Which words were used with these letters? Which other letter(s) could each one be confused with?**

N for ....*November*.... ..*M*.          B for ...............................  ............

S for ...............................  ............          Y for ...............................  ............

T for ...............................  ............          P for ...............................  ............

D for ...............................  ............          M for ...............................  ............

Notice how the speakers in Recording 7.2 clarified difficult numbers:

*that's* + using single digits

saying the numbers in a different way

**2  What did they say to clarify these numbers?**

**a**  22 (double two) .........................................................

**b**  0 (oh)          .........................................................

**c**  16 (sixteen)          .........................................................

**d**  35,850 (thirty-five thousand eight hundred and fifty)

.........................................................

7.2  **Listen again and check.**

**3  Practise with a partner. Say these numbers in two ways, clarifying the second time.**

*phone numbers* (remember to pause between groups)

a  56 22 14          b  202 663 412          c  7079 888 149

*other numbers*

d  415          e  18,888          f  614,260

## Practice

**Do the role plays in Communication activities.**

STUDENT A: turn to page 60.
STUDENT B: turn to page 67.

# Lesson B

- Checking details

**Read this text and fill in the gaps using these words.**

numbers   spell   stressing   single   common

When people leave a message, they often clarify it by (1)............*stressing*............
key words. They also (2)............................ out difficult words, and if the
letters are confusing, they clarify them by using a (3)............................ word
or name (e.g. D for David). It is possible to make difficult (4)............................
clearer by saying them in a different way or using (5)............................
digits, such as 'three seven' for 'thirty-seven'. But people don't always think
about these things – so you have to check the details.

## Listening 1

7.3  **Look at the following questions which can be used to clarify details.
Listen to three messages and decide which two questions go with each
message. Write the number of the message next to the questions.**

a ...2.. How do you spell the name of the town?

........................................................................................................

b ......... Sorry, was that 17 or 70?

........................................................................................................

c ......... Was that A for Amsterdam, J for John?

........................................................................................................

d ......... Could you repeat that, please – the price?

........................................................................................................

e ......... Sorry, but could you say the model number again more slowly?

........................................................................................................

f ......... Sorry, what was that – the check-in time?

........................................................................................................

7.4  **Listen to the complete conversations and check.**

## Listening 2

 7.4 **Listen to the complete conversations again and write the answers to the questions in Listening 1.**

## Language focus

### Pronunciation: intonation

 7.5 **1 Listen to these questions and repeat them. Does the voice rise** ➚ **or fall** ➘ **at the end of each question?**

1 How do you spell that?
2 Could you repeat that, please?
3 Sorry, but could you say that again more slowly?
4 Sorry, what was that?
5 Sorry, was that 17 or 70?
6 Was that A for Amsterdam or H for Harry?

**2 Practise conversations like the ones below with a partner, paying particular attention to intonation. Use these alternatives:**

30/13   I/Y   V/B   9/5   18/80   F/S

A: 17.
B: Was that 17 or 70?
A: 17, that's one seven.
B: OK, thanks.

B: H.
A: Sorry, was that H for Harry or A for Amsterdam?
B: H for Harry.
A: Right, thank you.

"Mr. Cosgrove has stepped away from his desk. May I take a message?"

## Practice

**Do the role plays in Communication activities.**
   STUDENT A: turn to page 60.
   STUDENT B: turn to page 67.

## Language summary

**See page 80 for a summary of the language you have learnt in this unit.**

# 8 | Consolidation Plus

## (Units 5 – 7)

## Listening

 8.1

**1 Listen to three conversations and tick (✓) the correct message for each one.**

**1**
a Jo Brant called. Please e-mail info about next meeting. ☐
b Joe Brandt called. Please fax info about the conference. ☐

**2**
a Paula Rogers from letstravel.com — she'll call back. ☐
b Pauline Richards from travelwithus.com — could you call her back? ☐

**3**
a Jackie phoned – can't come to the meeting tomorrow. ☐
b Jack phoned – can't come to the meeting this afternoon. ☐

8.2

**2 Listen to someone leaving a message and note it down. Then write it out clearly.**

**NOTES**

## Language focus

**1 Put these lines in the correct order to make a conversation.**

....... Yes, could you try Zeta in Sales? She might know.

..1.. Could you put me through to Jacob in Accounts, please?

....... Would you like me to take a message?

....... His line's busy at the moment. Can someone else help?

....... Just a moment while I get a pen.

....... Sorry. Her line's engaged, too.

....... Oh, yes, please. That's very kind of you.

....... Oh, dear … it is rather urgent.

**2 Now practise the conversation with a partner, paying attention to pronunciation.**

# Practice

**1  Practise this conversation in pairs. Take turns to play each role.**

**STUDENT A**                    **STUDENT B**

Answer the phone.

Give your name. Ask to speak to Mr Bosnic in IT.

Say Mr Bosnic can't take the call. Give a reason.

Say it's urgent.

Offer to take a message.

Accept the offer.

Ask B to wait while you prepare.

**2  Now practise a similar conversation.**
   **STUDENT A: turn to page 61.**
   **STUDENT B: turn to page 68.**

# New language

If you don't know the person the caller is asking for, you can say:

*I'm sorry, but I don't know anyone of that name.*
*I'm afraid you've made a mistake. There's no one of that name here.*

If there is no department of that name, you can say:

*I'm afraid we don't have a … Department. Would you like to speak to …?*

If you make a call and think you have made a mistake, you can say:

*I'm sorry. I've made a mistake.*
*Sorry, I'll check the name and number.*

**Now do the role play on pages 61 and 68 again. This time use the language above to help you remain calm and polite. Take turns to play each role.**

**See page 80 for a summary of the new language you have learnt in this unit.**

# 9 Communication problems

## Lesson A
- Responding to problems
- Dealing with speakers who are difficult to understand
- Dealing with technical problems

What can make people difficult to understand during a phone call?
Make a list of things (e.g. a strong accent) and then discuss with
a partner.

## Listening 1

 9.1

**Listen to extracts from five conversations. Write the number of the
conversation which includes:**

an address ............ an appointment ............ an invitation ............
an explanation ............ travel details ............

## Listening 2

9.1

**Listen again. What did the speakers say when they couldn't understand?
Fill in the gaps.**

**1**
**a** I'm sorry, but ........................................................ what you're saying.
**b** I ........................................................, I'm afraid.

**2**
**a** Can you ........................................, please? I can't hear you very well.
**b** I ........................ hear ................................. I think
........................ got ........................ .

**3**
**a** Would you ........................................, please?
**b** No, I still ........................................ .

**4**
**a** ........................................, please?
**b** I'm sorry, but ........................................ for me.

**5**
**a** Sorry, ........................................ .
**b** No, sorry, ........................................ .

## Language focus

**1  Look back at the 'a' sentences in Listening 2. Which one(s) can you say when someone is:**

1  not explaining clearly?
2  speaking with a strong accent?
3  speaking fast?
4  having problems with a mobile phone?
5  not speaking loudly enough?

**Discuss with a partner.**

**2  Notice the position of *still* in the sentences from Listening 2.
Add *still* to these sentences.**

1  You're speaking too fast.
2  I can't hear anything.
3  I don't know what you mean.
4  The line is bad.
5  I haven't found what I'm looking for.

*"Can you hear me now?"*

**Fill in the gaps with *before* and *after* to complete this rule about the position of *still*.**

We put *still* _____ the verb *to be* and _____ modals and auxiliaries.

## Practice

9.2

**1  Listen to the three speakers and respond appropriately in the pauses.**

**2  Practise this conversation in pairs. Take turns to play each role.**

**STUDENT A**

Give an address and phone number but speak softly.

Repeat what you said, but not loudly enough.

Say you're sorry ...

**STUDENT B**

Ask the other person to speak up.

Use a sentence with *still*.

# Lesson B

- Dealing with someone who can't
understand you

**What can you do if the person you're talking to can't understand you?**
**Look at the list of things you can do and decide which is best.**

- Say you're sorry and say goodbye.
- Ask to speak to someone else.
- Say you will call again.
- Put the phone down.

**With a partner, discuss what else you can do in this situation.**

## Listening 1

9.3  **Listen to how the calls you heard in Lesson A continue. Write the number(s) of the conversations in which the person who isn't understood:**

offers to spell something .........
says they'll communicate in some other way ......... .........
says they will phone again ......... .........

## Listening 2

9.3 **Rewrite these sentences from the conversations, putting the words in the correct order. Then listen again and check.**

1  in there your Italian who anyone office speaks is?

.........................................................................................................

2  you call back I'll

.........................................................................................................

3  with send an I'll details e-mail the all you

.........................................................................................................

4  for it slowly I'll out you spell

.........................................................................................................

5  going off again later and now I'm to try ring

.........................................................................................................

## Language focus

**Look at some more sentences that you can use when someone doesn't understand you (1–5). Match them to the appropriate responses (a–e). There may be more than one possibility.**

1 I'll send a fax with all the information.
2 I know – why don't I send you an e-mail?
3 Is there anyone else I could talk to?
4 I'll ask my boss to phone you in the morning.
5 Could you ring me and see if we get a better line?

a Yes … hold on a moment.
b Thanks very much.
c OK, good idea.
d Yes, of course I will.
e That would be helpful. Thanks.

### Pronunciation: chunking

9.4

1 **Mark the chunks in the exchanges above. Are there any that you can't divide into chunks? Discuss with a partner. Then listen and check.**

2 **Work with a different partner. Look at Transcript 9.3 on page 95. Practise one of the conversations, paying particular attention to chunking.**

## Practice

1 **Practise this conversation in pairs. Take turns to play each role.**

STUDENT A

Ask what B wants.

Ask B to speak more slowly (or more loudly).

Use a sentence with *still*.

Respond appropriately.

STUDENT B

Give a time and date for a meeting but speak too fast (or too quietly).

Repeat what you said but not slowly (or loudly) enough.

Think of a way to deal with the problem.

2 **Work with a different partner. Write down two pieces of information (e.g. an e-mail address, the prices of some products) to give to your partner. Have 'problem' conversations, making up the difficulties yourselves. Take turns to give and receive the information.**

## Language summary

**See page 81 for a summary of the language you have learnt in this unit.**

## Lesson A

- Making appointments
  and arrangements

---

**With which of these people would you normally make:**

- an appointment?  • an arrangement?  • either?

  boss  friend  colleague  husband/wife  business partner
  accountant  bank manager

**Discuss with a partner.**

---

## Listening 1

 10.1

**Listen to three conversations. What is the relationship between the two people in each one? Write the number of the conversation next to the people.**

secretary and client ...........
boss's PA (personal assistant) and employee ........
colleagues ..........

**Are the people making an appointment or an arrangement?**

## Listening 2

10.1

**Listen again to Conversations 1 and 2 and fill in the gaps in these lines.**

**1**
Not bad, but I think we .................................................................................... soon
.................................................................. it.
OK. .............................. lunchtime tomorrow?
Yes, fine. ........................................................ in the canteen at 1.15.

**2**
It's Imran Shah here. Could I ...........................................................................
to ...................... him some time this week?
Just a moment. I'll .............................. his .......................... .
................................................ . Friday 14th at 2.30?
Yes, .............................................. . Friday, 2.30.
May I ask what ........................................ ?

**Compare your answers with a partner. Listen again and check.**

## Language focus

10.1  **Fill in the table with phrases from Conversations 1 and 2. Then listen again to Conversation 3 and complete the table.**

*To say you want to meet/see someone*

...................................................................................................................................................................

...................................................................................................................................................................

...................................................................................................................................................................

...................................................................................................................................................................

*To suggest a time and day*

...................................................................................................................................................................

...................................................................................................................................................................

*To confirm a time and day*

...................................................................................................................................................................

...................................................................................................................................................................

...................................................................................................................................................................

*To ask about the subject of the meeting*

...................................................................................................................................................................

...................................................................................................................................................................

## Practice

**Practise this conversation in pairs. Take turns to play each role.**

**STUDENT A**

You are Mr Moya's PA.
Answer the phone.

Offer a time/day.

Ask what it's about.

Confirm the details.

Acknowledge B's thanks.

**STUDENT B**

Say who you are and ask for an appointment with Mr Moya.

Agree.

Say what it's about.

Say thank you.

Say goodbye.

# Lesson B

- Confirming, changing and cancelling
  appointments and arrangements
- Checking details

**Match the dates/times on the left with the ones on the right.**

| | | | |
|---|---|---|---|
| **1** | 17.35 | **a** | September 23rd |
| **2** | 8.45 | **b** | 6 June 2003 |
| **3** | 12/10/05 | **c** | twenty-five to six in the evening |
| **4** | 6/6/03 | **d** | quarter to nine in the morning |
| **5** | 24.00 | **e** | October 12th 2005 |
| **6** | 07.15 | **f** | midnight |
| **7** | 23/09 | **g** | January 1st |
| **8** | New Year's Day | **h** | quarter past seven in the morning |

**Now write down three more dates/times. Work in pairs. Take turns to dictate your dates/times to your partner. Your partner should write them down. Check together at the end.**

## Listening 1

10.2  **Listen to three conversations. Complete the sentences with these words:**

> change    confirm    cancel

**1** The caller wants to ......................................... the time.

**2** The caller wants to ......................................... the appointment.

**3** The caller wants to ......................................... the appointment.

## Listening 2

**Look at these extracts from the three conversations. Put the lines in the correct order.**

**1**

........ It was 1.15 – in the canteen.

........ That's OK. Bye.

..*1*.. I just wanted to check the time of our meeting tomorrow. Was it 1.15 or 1.30?

........ OK. Sorry about that.

"No, Thursday's out. How about never –
is never good for you?"

**2**

........ It's quite all right. Don't worry about it. Would you like to make another appointment?

........ Yes, I remember.

........ I do apologise, but I have to cancel it.

........ No, I'll just cancel it for now.

...*1*... I made an appointment to see Mr Fischer on Friday.

**3**

........ Yes, Wednesday 28th at 11.30.

........ Yes, that's right. I'm really sorry, but could we make it a different day?

........ Yes ... Ms Chen?

........ Wednesday 28th?

...*1*... I have an appointment with Mr Cohen next Thursday – the 29th – at 9.30.

........ That's great. Thank you very much.

........ That's all right. Just a moment ... What about Wednesday instead?

10.2  **Listen again and check.**

## Language focus

**Look back at the lines you ordered in Listening 2. Underline the phrases used to check and change appointments and arrangements.**

### Pronunciation: stress

**Work with a partner. Mark the main stress on the phrases you underlined. Then practise saying them.**

10.3 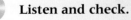 **Listen and check.**

## Practice

**Do the role plays in Communication activities.**
   STUDENT A: turn to page 61.
   STUDENT B: turn to page 68.

## Language summary

**See page 82 for a summary of the language you have learnt in this unit.**

# 11 | Recorded information

## Lesson A

- Understanding recorded
  information

---

**Look at these statements. Tick (✓) *agree, disagree* or *not sure*.
Discuss with a partner.**

|  | agree | disagree | not sure |
|---|---|---|---|
| • These days a lot of information is recorded. | ......... | ......... | ......... |
| • Listening to recorded information is harder than listening to a person. | ......... | ......... | ......... |
| • There are some advantages if information is recorded. | ......... | ......... | ......... |

## Listening 1

**Look at the telephone keypad. Draw a
line from each box to the correct key.**

( hash/square key )    ( star key )

11.1  **Now listen to a telephone announcement. You want information
about special offers on notebook computers only. Listen and put the
buttons on the keypad in the order that you need to press them.**

1 ............... 2 ............... 3 ............... 4 ...............

## Listening 2

11.2  **1 Listen to three pieces of recorded information and tick (✓) what
each one is about.**

**1**
**a** train times from Brussels to Amsterdam ........
**b** train times from Amsterdam to Brussels ........

**2**
**a** special offers on computer equipment ........
**b** a telephone message service ........

**3**
**a** opening hours ........
**b** an emergency service ........

**2 Listen again and look at the notes someone has made for each piece of information. Correct the mistakes.**

**1**
Train info – Amsterdam to Brussels. Every hr on the hr from 5 am + 7.30, 8.30, 9.30. Journey time 2 hrs 40 mins (approx).

**2**
Message Plus – pay next 9 days, receive 2 wks free + 2 mths @ £33.99 per mth. Prize draw – £2,000 worth of computer equipment.

**3**
TVT – closed till Mon Feb 7th then open Mon to Sat 8 am to 6 pm + Sun 8 am to 4 pm. In emergency, call 08000 276 923.

## Language focus

Most people find it helpful to use abbreviations and short forms of words when they make notes.

**1 Look at these abbreviations from the notes in Listening 2 and write the full forms next to them.**

| | | | |
|---|---|---|---|
| info | ........................................ | mth(s) | ........................................ |
| hr(s) | ........................................ | @ | ........................................ |
| am | ........................................ | Mon | ........................................ |
| mins | ........................................ | Feb | ........................................ |
| approx | ........................................ | Sat | ........................................ |
| wks | ........................................ | pm | ........................................ |

**2 What do these notes mean? Write them out in full.**

**1** Tim arriving next week – Tues 10am approx

........................................................................................................................

**2** Office opening hrs: Mon-Fri 8am-6pm, Sat 9am-1pm

........................................................................................................................

**3** Price info: for 6 wks only, laptop computers @£995/€1,495

........................................................................................................................

## Practice

**Do the role play in Communication activities.**
STUDENT A: turn to page 62.
STUDENT B: turn to page 68.

# Lesson B

- Asking for and giving information
- Checking you have understood

---

Read these sentences and mark them A (asking for information),
G (giving information) or C (checking information).

1  Could I have some information about ...?    *A*
2  OK ... the address is ...    ........
3  Could you repeat that, please?    ........
4  Right, the number you wanted is ...    ........
5  I'm enquiring about ...    ........
6  I'd like to speak to someone about ...    ........
7  Was that 14 or 40?    ........
8  Could I just check I've got that right?    ........
9  I'd like to ask about ...    ........
10  We are open from nine to eight every day.    ........

---

## Listening 1

11.3  Listen to this conversation about notebook computers and fill in the information.

**NOTEBOOKS**
Model: ...............................................................................
Special price (without VAT): ................................................
VAT: ..................................................................................
Total: .................................................................................
Offer valid until : ...............................................................

## Listening 2

11.4  1 Listen to two conversations. What does the caller want to know about in each case?

1  ...........................................................................................

2  ...........................................................................................

11.4  **2 Listen again and fill in the gaps in these lines from the conversations.**

**1**

Oh hello. _____ your advertisement in *The Post*.

Could you tell me _____ your offers on mobile phones?

_____ 1-5 or1-9?

_____ 07976 15358.

**2**

I'd like to _____ .

Well, I _____ help.

OK. _____ to get there from the station, please?

_____ the address, please?

## Language focus

**Match the sentences (1–5) with a suitable response (a–e).**

1 The reference number is 1457RT.
2 I'd like to speak to someone about an invoice, please.
3 Could you just repeat the number, please?
4 I'd like some more information about the programme, please.
5 Was that Tuesday or Thursday?

a I'll put you through to Accounts.
b It's Thursday 26th.
c Was that T for Tom or D for David?
d Yes, it's 09763 425713.
e Well, I can probably help.

### Pronunciation: intonation

11.5  **Look at the sentences above. Decide if the intonation rises ➝ or falls ➝ at the end of them. Practise the exchanges with a partner. Then listen and check.**

## Practice

**Do the role plays in Communication activities.**
STUDENT A: turn to page 62.
STUDENT B: turn to page 68.

## Language summary

See page 83 for a summary of the language you have learnt in this unit.

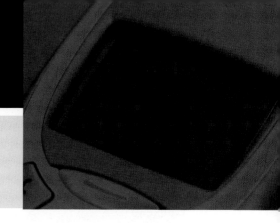

# 12 Messages 3

## Lesson A

- Understanding recorded messages
- Leaving a message on an answering machine / voice mail

What do you remember from Units 6 and 7 about leaving messages? What things are important?

For leaving a recorded message, what things stay the same? What things are different? Discuss with a partner.

## Listening 1

12.1 Listen to six answering machine / voice mail messages. What do they ask the caller to do? Number the instructions in the correct order.

Leave your name and number. ........     Leave a message or send a fax. ........
Phone again or contact a website. ........     Press a button on your keypad. ........
Call a different number. ........     Leave your name and address. ........

## Listening 2

12.2 1 Listen to the three messages people left on the answering machines / voice mails in Listening 1. In which two does the speaker clarify the information?

12.2 2 Use the phrases in the box to fill in the gaps in these lines from the clearer messages. Then listen again and check.

> 3 A for Apple    that's Stephan with PH    one eight
> that's 0783 22 6372    all one word    that's S dot FREUND, F-R-E-U-N-D
> that's R-A-S for Sugar-H-I-D    S-T-O-C-K-T-O-N

1
This is Stephan Freund, ........................................ , wanting to speak to
Ms Sanchez. Call me on 0783 double 2 6372, ........................................ ,
or e-mail me. The address is s.freund@jkint.com, ........................................ ,
at jkint dot com. It's quite urgent. Thank you.

2
Yes. My name's Ali Rashid, that's Ali – A-L-I, Rashid – ........................................ ,
address 3A, ........................................ , 18, ........................................ , Broadway,
........................................ , Stockton, ........................................ , TN23 6EZ.

## Language focus

Remember that when listening to a recorded message, the listener has none of the help which is possible when taking a message from a person, like asking for repetition or clarification.

This means that when you leave a message on an answering machine / voice mail you have to be even more careful about speaking clearly and clarifying any important details.

Sometimes you expect to hear a machine, so you can prepare your message in advance – perhaps even write it down so you can read it out.

It's always a good idea to be as prepared as you can be.

**Notice the different clarifying techniques which the speakers in Listening 2 used. Work with a partner and make a list of the different techniques, with one example of each.**

| *Techniques* | *Examples* |
|---|---|
| *Clarifying difficult spelling.* | *That's Stephan with P.H.* |
| *Repeating the whole number.* | |
| | |
| | |
| | |
| | |

## Practice

1  **Prepare a short message to leave on someone's answering machine / voice mail. Spell out your name and give your telephone number and a time when they can call you back. Practise with a partner, paying particular attention to each other's pronunciation.**

   **Pair up with a new partner and 'leave' your message. Your partner should write it down. Then swap roles. At the end, check the messages with your partner.**

2  **Do the role plays in Communication activities.**
   **STUDENT A: turn to page 63.**
   **STUDENT B: turn to page 69.**

*"I'm sorry but my fax and answering machine can't get to the phone right now, but if you'd like to leave a message they'll get back to you as soon as possible."*

# Lesson B

- Responding to messages
- Using abbreviations

**Look at these text messages. Discuss what they mean with a partner.**

- Want 2 tlk? Cll now
- Cll me this pm B4 6
- RU busy tonite? How about mtg?

## Listening 1

12.3 **Listen to three messages. Number the descriptions of each message in the order that you hear them.**

someone wanting to arrange some interviews ........

someone confirming travel arrangements ........

someone agreeing to change the day of a meeting ........

## Listening 2

12.3 **Listen again and tick (✓) the phrases you hear.**

Thanks for calling me back. ........          Thanks for phoning back. ........

Thanks for your message. ........          I've just got your e-mail. ........

I've just got your message. ........          I've just got your fax. ........

I'm just returning his call. ........          Thanks for getting back to me. ........

## Language focus

### Pronunciation: stress and intonation

12.4 **Practise saying all the sentences above with a partner, paying particular attention to stress and intonation. Then listen and check.**

1 **Fill in the gaps with an appropriate word or phrase from the sentences above.**

Thanks for your ..................................          I've just got your ..................................

Thanks for ..................................          ..................................

..................................          ..................................

..................................          I'm just ..................................

**Notice the different structures. In which of the sentences does *just* mean *only* and in which does it mean a *short time ago*?**

**2** **In Unit 11 you looked at some abbreviations and short forms. Look at the messages below and underline the abbreviations. What do you think they mean?**

**1**
Alex – Hans called.
Could you call him back
asap re meeting next Tues
am?

**2**
John – Fiona rang. She needs to change her appt from Mon to Fri, if poss. Call her back on 08795 770722.

**4**
Hello, Juan. Could you
give me a ring about the
Sales Conf? I need to
check the nos.
Michel

**3**
Hi, Bill. I need to speak to you
this pm if poss about the project.
I'm in the Accounts dept till 6.30.
Tamara

**Now match the abbreviations in box A with one of the words or phrases in box B and look back at the messages to check.**

| A | | | | B | | |
|---|---|---|---|---|---|---|
| | asap | Fri | | | Monday | appointment |
| | re | poss | | | Tuesday | department |
| | Tues | pm | | | Friday | numbers |
| | am | dept | | | morning | regarding (= about) |
| | appt | conf | | | afternoon | possible |
| | Mon | nos | | | conference | as soon as possible |

## Practice

**Using the four messages in Language focus above as your starting point, practise conversations with a partner.**

**For 1 and 2, Student A turn to page 63. Student B respond appropriately.**
**For 3 and 4, Student B turn to page 70. Student A respond appropriately.**

## Language summary

**See page 84 for a summary of the language you have learnt in this unit.**

## 13.1 Listening

**Listen to this conversation. Tick (✓) the correct answers.**

1 The caller wants information about
   a pension schemes ........
   b investments ........
   c taxation ........

2 The caller needs to speak to a
   a financial adviser ........
   b careers adviser ........
   c customer services adviser ........

3 She makes an appointment for
   a Monday ........
   b Thursday ........
   c Tuesday ........

4 The appointment time is
   a 2.30 ........
   b 3.30 ........
   c 4.30 ........

5 The name of the adviser is
   a Mr Schulz ........
   b Mr Schmidt ........
   c Mr Schlitz ........

## Language focus

**Fill in the gaps in these sentences.**

1 I'd .................................... to .................................... an ....................................
   to .................................... Mr Boric.

2 How .................................... next week some time?

3 .................................... I ask what it's .................................... ?

4 .................................... I just .................................... I've got that
   .................................... ?

## Practice

**1  Practise this conversation with a partner. Take turns to play each role.**

| STUDENT A | STUDENT B |
|---|---|
| | Answer the phone. |
| Introduce yourself. | |
| | Greet A. |
| Ask for an appointment with Ms Lopez. | |
| | Suggest a time/day. |
| Say the time/day is not possible. Apologise. | |
| | Accept the apology. Offer a new time/day. |
| Ask B to repeat. Say the line is bad. | |
| | Repeat the time/day. |
| Agree. Ask for the address. | |
| | Give the address. |
| Ask for clarification of any difficult spellings/numbers. | |
| | Clarify where necessary. |
| Confirm details of appointment. | |
| | Say goodbye. |
| Say goodbye. | |

**2  Do role play 1 in Communication activities.**

STUDENT A: turn to page 64.          STUDENT B: turn to page 70.

## New language

If you can't find a suitable time to meet or can't reach agreement about something else, you can say:

> *I'm sorry. I think we'll have to leave it for now.*
> *It seems it's just not possible at the moment.*
> *Let's try again in a few days/weeks.*

The other person can say:

> *That's OK. / That's all right.*

**Do role play 2 in Communication activities.**

STUDENT A: turn to page 64.          STUDENT B: turn to page 70.

**See page 85 for a summary of the new language you have learnt in this unit.**

## Lesson A

- Understanding telephone conferences
- Presenting information
- Expressing opinions
- Agreeing and disagreeing

**Read this text about telephone conferences and discuss the questions below with a partner.**

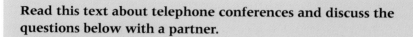**A telephone conference** is a meeting between a number of people which is conducted on the telephone. The participants can be anywhere in the world, but it is important to try to choose a time which is suitable for all of them. There are many advantages to telephone conferences – they can be immediate and efficient, and they can obviously save a good deal of time and expense. There are also disadvantages, however. It can be difficult to have an organised meeting when you can't see people's faces, and some people find the idea of speaking on the phone to more than one person at a time very strange indeed.

1  Why do companies hold telephone conferences?
2  What are some of the problems?
3  Would you like to take part in a telephone conference?

**Read this information from a telephone book. It shows time differences in different countries. (GMT =** *Greenwich Mean Time.***)**

| **Brazil**<br>GMT – 3 hours | **Japan**<br>GMT + 9 hours | **Russia (West)**<br>GMT + 3 hours |
|---|---|---|
| **China**<br>GMT + 8 hours | **Mexico**<br>GMT – 6 hours | **South Korea**<br>GMT + 9 hours |
| **France**<br>GMT + 1 hour | **Poland**<br>GMT + 1 hour | **USA (East)**<br>GMT – 5 hours |

**If it is midday in London (GMT), what time is it in the following places?**

New York    ................    São Paulo    ................
Tokyo       ................    Seoul        ................
Warsaw      ................

## Listening 1

14.1

**1 Listen to the beginning of a telephone conference.
Tick (✓) the places where the participants are.**

| | | |
|---|---|---|
| Mexico City ......... | New York ......... | São Paulo ......... |
| London ......... | Paris ......... | Warsaw ......... |
| Moscow ......... | Beijing ......... | Tokyo ......... |
| Seoul ......... | Sydney ......... | |

**2 What problems did the participants have?**

**3 What time is it in Seoul? What time is it in the other cities? Use the
information opposite and suggest a better time for them to have the
conference.**

## Listening 2

The participants in Listening 1 have now chosen a suitable time and have
prepared for a successful conference.

The participants all work for the same international software company
(CIS) in different parts of the world. They are having a conference to
discuss the best way to improve the English of their employees.

14.2

**1 Listen to the first part of the conference. Fill in the table with the
correct job or company department and city for each person.**

| Name | Job/Department | City |
|---|---|---|
| Michel Lefevre | | |
| Glen Parsons | | |
| Susi Tan | | |
| Lola Sanchez | | |
| Ivan Karpov | | |

14.3

**2 Listen to the second part of the conference. Tick (✓) the options
each person mentions – even if they don't agree with them.**

| Name | In-company teacher | Lunchtime/ Evening course | Staff to English-speaking country |
|---|---|---|---|
| Michel Lefevre | | | |
| Glen Parsons | | | |
| Susi Tan | | | |
| Lola Sanchez | | | |
| Ivan Karpov | | | |

## Language focus

**1 Match each word (1–6) with a definition (a–f).**

| | | | |
|---|---|---|---|
| 1 | to chair | **a** | list of items for a meeting |
| 2 | key staff | **b** | good value for money |
| 3 | motivated | **c** | to manage a meeting |
| 4 | options | **d** | important/senior employees |
| 5 | cost-effective | **e** | interested/keen |
| 6 | agenda | **f** | alternatives |

**2 Look at these phrases from Listening 2. Mark them P (presenting information), O (expressing an opinion), A (agreeing) or D (disagreeing).**

1  I'm A and I'm chairing this meeting.          ..........
2  Well, personally, I think the best solution is ...          ..........
3  I certainly agree.          ..........
4  I completely agree with you.          ..........
5  Well, in my opinion, ...          ..........
6  I'm not sure I agree with that.          ..........
7  I feel that generally ...          ..........
8  I work in Human Resources.          ..........
9  That sounds like a very good idea to me.          ..........
10  I don't agree that ...          ..........
11  I've organised this meeting to discuss ...          ..........
12  I really think it would be better to ...          ..........

## Pronunciation

14.4

**Look at the phrases again and practise saying them with a partner. Then listen and check.**

## Practice

**Take turns to give an opinion about the following topics. Your partner should either agree or disagree.**

### Example

• working with computers
A: *I really think working with computers is very unhealthy.*
B: *I completely agree with you.*

| | | |
|---|---|---|
| • mobile phones | • e-mail | • answering machines |
| • using public phones | • taking messages | • using abbreviations |

# Lesson B

• Taking part in a telephone conference

## Preparation

You are going to take part in a telephone conference with four other people. You all work for the international software company CIS. The conference is to discuss the English language training options for your company.

Read your role card and the agenda below and check any words you are not sure about.

Make some notes about what you want to say.

Think about what the other participants might say and whether you will agree or disagree.

STUDENT A: turn to page 64.
STUDENT B: turn to page 70.
STUDENT C: turn to page 71.
STUDENT D: turn to page 72.
STUDENT E: turn to page 73.

## Agenda

1  Introduction of each participant.
2  Each participant, starting with the Chair, briefly presents their own opinion.
3  The Chair invites the participants to have a general discussion.
4  Participants vote on the best option.
5  Any other business.

## Practice

Now have the telephone conference.
The Chair will lead the conference.
Take notes on what each person says.
Remember to try to use some of the language you practised in Lesson A, but the most important thing is to communicate effectively.

## Language summary

See page 85 for a summary of the language you have learnt in this unit.

**1 Put a cross (✗) by the sentence which is not correct as a way of introducing yourself on the phone.**

1 This is Marcella. ........
2 It's Marcella speaking. ........
3 I am Marcella. ........
4 It's Marcella here. ........

**2 Write down three ways to ask to speak to someone on the phone.**

......................................................................................................

......................................................................................................

......................................................................................................

**3 Fill in the gaps in these sentences from the end of a call.**

1 Give my ............................... to Freddie.

2 Thanks for ............................... me back.

3 ............................... a nice weekend.

4 ............................... to you soon.

**4 Match each phrase (1–5) with the correct definition (a–e).**

1 pick up the phone    **a** wait
2 call back    **b** connect
3 put someone through    **c** answer
4 hold on    **d** end the call
5 put the phone down    **e** return the call

**5 Write down three ways to offer to take a message for someone.**

......................................................................................................

......................................................................................................

......................................................................................................

**6 Complete these word maps with two suitable nouns or noun phrases about telephoning.**

Example

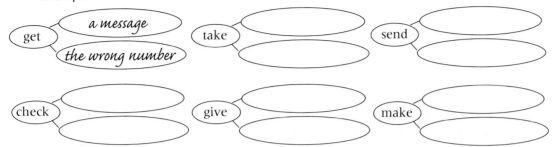

**7 Put these words in the correct order to make sentences.**

1 Jan speak IT could to I please in? ..................................................................................

2 to thanks back getting me for .........................................................................................

3 call returning just his am I .............................................................................................

4 you still understand don't are I saying what...............................................................

5 to message like you a would leave? ...........................................................................

6 possible as as see soon need I to her..........................................................................

**8 Underline the key words in these messages.**

1 Could you fax the details today?

2 The boss needs to cancel the meeting on Tuesday.

3 Klara wants to change her appointment to a later date.

4 I need some information about the sales conference.

5 Could you contact Pedro before five this afternoon?

**9 What do these abbreviations mean? Write the full forms.**

| | | |
|---|---|---|
| 1 asap ..................... | 5 no | ..................... |
| 2 re ..................... | 6 appt | ..................... |
| 3 conf ..................... | 7 dept | ..................... |
| 4 poss ..................... | 8 am | ..................... |

**10 Put these lines in the correct order to make a conversation.**

.......... Oh, yes. Thanks very much.

...1... Good morning. Could I speak to Jack in Marketing, please?

.......... I think we've got a bad line then. Shall I call you again?

.......... Oh, hello, Jack. It's Ken.

.......... Certainly. I'll put you through.

.......... Is that any better?

.......... Hello, Ken ... er, sorry. Can you speak up? I can't hear you.

.10. That's OK.

.......... No. I still can't hear you properly.

.......... Jack here.

# Communication activities

## STUDENT A

## 2   Beginning a call (Lesson B)     page 13

**1**
**Student B will call you.**

Answer the phone (your company name is ABC Software).
After B introduces him/herself, check the name.
After B has introduced him/herself again, ask him/her to wait.

**2**
**Call Student B.**

Introduce yourself (you are Nicky Richards). Ask for Peter.
When B checks, clarify who you are / say why you're calling and ask for Peter again.

**Now think up more names of people and companies, and ways of clarifying who you are. Practise more calls with B. Take turns to answer the phone.**

## 3   Ending a call (Lesson B)     page 17

**1**
**You are ending a call with Student B. Student B speaks first. Include the following in your conversation:**

Thank B (they called you).
Agree to the request B makes.
Ask B to give your regards to John.

**2**
**You are ending a call with Student B. You speak first. Include the following in your conversation:**

Ask B to book a table at The Black Rose restaurant for next Wednesday at 1 pm.
Offer to photocopy the report and bring it with you.
You'll see B next Wednesday at 1 pm at The Black Rose restaurant.

# 4    Consolidation Plus (Units 1–3)

page 19

**Student B will call you.**

Answer the phone with the name of your company (Computer World).
Your phone number is 0207 316549.
This is part of an alphabetical list of all the names and extension numbers of
people who work in your company:

| | |
|---|---|
| DAWSON, Pete | 761 |
| GREAVES, Sophie | 943 |
| HENDERSON, Kate | 265 |

# 5    Connecting people (Lesson B)

page 23

**In 1–4 you are the caller. Invent a name or use your own.**

**1**
Phone Kennedy Cars. You want to speak to Bob in the Customer Services
Department.
(If Bob is unavailable, say you'll ring back later.)

**2**
Call E20 Services. You want to speak to Rosa in Personnel.
(If Rosa is not available, say you'll ring back later.)

**3**
Call Datasolve. Introduce yourself. You want to speak to Yuki in the Sales
Department.
(If Yuki is unavailable, ask for the name of someone in the department you can
speak to.)

**4**
Ring R and R Rentals. Introduce yourself. You want to speak to someone in the
Marketing Department.
(If there is no one available, ask for the name of someone in the department you
can call later, and their direct line number.)

**In 5–8 you are answering the phone.**

**5**
You work for IT Systems. Answer the phone. Ask the caller to wait. Put them
through to Gloria.

**6**
You work for PR Products. Answer the phone. Ask the caller to wait. Ask the
caller what their name is. Say everyone is on the phone and ask the caller if they
want to hold on.

**7**

You work for Quicktech. Answer the phone. Ask the caller to wait. Check what their name is. Tell them that Pia is unavailable and ask if they want to speak to someone else.

**8**

You work for Halls. Answer the phone. The caller has got the wrong number/company – they want Henderson and Co. Continue in your role and make sure the caller realises they've got the wrong number/company – see how well they deal with the situation!

## 7   Messages 2 (Lesson A)page 29

**You are going to give two messages to Student B and take two messages from Student B.**

Work with another Student A to prepare your messages. Discuss the key words and any details that may be difficult for Student B.

Practise your messages with your partner.

Join Student B and give your messages. Then take Student B's messages. Make notes.

Then check each other's messages and discuss how well you gave them.

**1**

Your name is Jo Finch. You want to leave a message for Diego Fuentes. Your fax machine isn't working. You want him to send all faxes to 44 1295 783466 for the rest of this week.

**2**

Your name is Les Jarvis. You want to leave a message for Zaida Alpay. You made a mistake when you sent an e-mail to her yesterday. The price of the printer is $195, not $175.

## 7   Messages 2 (Lesson B)page 31

**You are going to give two messages to Student B and take two messages from Student B.**

Don't clarify the details in your messages until B asks you to.

When B thinks they have got the messages right, they will give the same messages to you, but they will clarify all the details.

You must check that B gives you exactly the same message that you gave before.

**1**

Your name is Georgie Eastman. You want to leave a message for Concha Munoz. You want her to know immediately that you couldn't get a reservation for her at The Plaza. She will be staying instead at The Grand, and the address is 44, Central Avenue. You will meet her there at ten o'clock in the morning.

**2**

Your name is Jackie Innis. You want to leave a message for Brad Durango. You're at the airport and have just heard that your flight is delayed. It is going to arrive at 16.40 instead of 14.20. If Brad Durango can't meet you, he needs to ring you as soon as possible on your mobile. The number is 07973482316.

## 8  Consolidation Plus (Units 5–7)  page 33

**Call Student B.**

Ask to be put through to Vince West in Marketing.

If B thinks Mr West isn't there, insist you want to speak to him. You know he works there.

If Student B tells you that you're wrong and gets angry, say goodbye. Put the phone down.

## 10  Appointments and arrangements (Lesson B) page 41

**You are going to make two calls to Student B and receive one call from Student B.**

**1**

Invent a name or use your own. Call Mr Klein's PA. Apologise and say you have to cancel your appointment – give the day and time. Say you don't want another appointment.

**2**

You are Ms Teser's secretary. Student B calls you. Offer a new time for B's appointment. Acknowledge B's apology and thanks, and finish the conversation.

**3**

You are Stevie Fleet. Call your colleague, Lindsay Castle, to check the details of your meeting. Confirm the details given and thank Lindsay. Finish the conversation.

## 11 Recorded information (Lesson A)     page 43

**Prepare to read the information below as clearly as you can to Student B. Pay attention to stress and chunking.**

When you are ready, take turns to read your information. B should note down the important information, using abbreviations if possible.

*This is MAM. Our offices are closed at the moment but you can call our 24-hour infoline on 07773 584 326. Or call again Monday to Friday between 8 am and 6 pm or Saturday between 8 am and 12 pm.*

## 11 Recorded information (Lesson B)     page 45

**Call Student B. Make notes during the calls and check that you have written the information you're given correctly.**

**1**
Call Rising Sun Travel. Ask about flight times from Tokyo to Sydney on Saturdays.

**2**
A new member of staff is starting work next week. Ring your colleague Pat and find out the name of the new member of staff and his/her extension number.

**Now Student B will call you and ask for information. Answer their questions using the following information. Give spellings where you think it is necessary/helpful.**

**3**
You are the Managing Director's secretary, Sam. Answer B's call. The meeting is at two o'clock tomorrow. It will probably last about an hour and a half. The person giving the presentation is Matt Fletcher.

**4**
You are Lesley. To get to your office from the station:
- turn left out of the station
- turn right at the traffic lights
- the office is the second large building on the left
  (it's a five-minute walk).

# 12 Messages 3 (Lesson A)
page 47

**Read the instructions below quickly and think briefly about what you are going to say. When you are ready, take turns to practise leaving messages on an answering machine / voice mail.**

When Student B gives you a cue like 'You've reached the voice mail of X. Please leave your message', give your message.

When B is giving a message, note down the important points.

Check your notes and messages together when you have finished.

**1**

Invent a name, address, company and phone number, or use your own. You want some information about the latest products as soon as possible. Give your name, address and phone number.

**2**

Invent a name or use your own. You work for goeurope.com. Call and leave a message for Ms Patel. There's a flight to Berlin from London City Airport at 08.30 and another at 10.45. Ask her to call back. Give your name and number.

**3**

Invent a name or use your own. Call your colleague. Say who you are and ask if you can change your meeting tomorrow to half an hour later. Say when your colleague can call you back.

# 12 Messages 3 (Lesson B)
page 49

**You are going to make two calls to Student B and receive two calls from Student B.**

**1**

You are Alex. Tell your colleague, Hans, that you have to cancel next Tuesday's meeting as you have been called away to Hong Kong. Suggest a new date for your meeting.

**2**

You are John. Call Fiona and offer her a new time for the appointment on Friday.

**3**

You are Tamara. Respond to Bill's call.

**4**

You are Michel. Respond to Juan's call.

## 13 **Consolidation Plus (Units 9–12)** page 51

**You are going to receive one call from Student B and make one call to Student B.**

**1**

You are Ms Lo's PA. Student B calls you. Offer B an appointment time/day and keep offering until you lose patience.

**2**

Invent a name or use your own. Phone Mr Prada's PA. Try to make an appointment with Mr Prada. You can't manage any of the times offered. Remain polite and say you will try again later.

## 14 **Telephone conferences (Lesson B)** page 55

## Participant 1 (Chair)

**Your name is Yodchai Singh. You are the Managing Director of the Bangkok branch of CIS. You have called a meeting to discuss the English language training options for your company. It is your job to:**

- make sure everyone takes turns to speak
- open the meeting up to a general discussion
- invite the participants to vote at the end of the discussion.

**You also need to give your own opinion. Your opinion is as follows:**

*The best option*

- private language schools in employees' home town

*Advantages*

- cheap
- requires little organisation

Notes

# Communication activities

## STUDENT B

## 2   Beginning a call (Lesson B) page 13

**1**
**Call Student A.**

Introduce yourself (you are Sam Nichols). Ask for Flora.
When A checks, clarify who you are / say why you're calling and ask for Flora again.

**2**
**Student A will call you.**

Answer the phone (your company name is Sun Travel).
After A introduces him/herself, check the name.
After A has introduced him/herself again, ask him/her to wait.

**Now think up more names of people and companies, and ways of clarifying who you are. Practise more calls with A. Take turns to answer the phone.**

## 3   Ending a call (Lesson B) page 17

**1**
**You are ending a call with Student A. You speak first. Include the following in your conversation:**

You called to tell A about tomorrow's meeting. It starts at 10.30.
Ask if A can arrive ten minutes early (there's something you want to discuss before the meeting).
Agree to the request A makes.

**2**
**You are ending a call with Student A. Student A speaks first. Include the following in your conversation:**

Thank A (they called you back). Agree to A's request.
Accept A's offer.
You'll see A next Wednesday at 1 pm at The Black Rose restaurant.

## 4   **Consolidation Plus (Units 1–3)** page 19

**Make a call to Student A.**

Call ZBD Insurance.
You want to speak to Dave English (extension number 637).
Check the name of the company.
Check their phone number – the number you want is 0207 315649.

## 5   **Connecting people (Lesson B)** page 23

**In 1–4 you are answering the phone.**

**1**

You work for Kennedy Cars. Answer the phone. Check the caller's name. Ask them to wait. Put them through to Bob.

**2**

You work for E20 Services. Answer the phone. Ask the caller to wait. Tell them Rosa is unavailable.

**3**

You work for Datasolve. Answer the phone. Ask the caller to wait. Check the caller's name. Tell them Yuki is busy but will ring back in five minutes. (If they ask to speak to someone else, suggest Ingrid, on extension 2895.)

**4**

You work for R and R Rentals. Answer the phone. Ask the caller to wait. Tell them there is no one available in the department. If they ask for a name and number, suggest Mr Parsons (452631).

**In 5–8 you are the caller. Invent a name or use your own.**

**5**

Ring IT Systems. Ask to speak to Gloria in Accounts.
(If they ask you to hold on because Gloria is busy, say you can't wait but will call back later.)

**6**

Ring PR Products. Ask to speak to someone in the Sales Department.
(If they ask you to hold on because there's no one available, say you will for a couple of minutes.)

**7**

Ring Quicktech. Introduce yourself. Ask for Pia in Marketing.
(If they ask you if you want to speak to someone else, say that you do.)

**8**

Call Henderson and Co. Ask for someone in the Human Resources department.
(If they ask you if you want to speak to someone else, say that you'll try again later, but you would like a name and number so you can call direct.)

## 7   Messages 2 (Lesson A)                    page 29

**You are going to give two messages to Student A and take two messages from Student A.**

Work with another Student B to prepare your messages. Discuss the key words and any details that may be difficult for Student A.

Practise your messages with your partner.

Join Student A and take their messages. Then give Student A your messages. Make notes.

Then check each other's messages and discuss how well you gave them.

**1**
Your name is Jon Street. You want to leave a message for Samad Abdul. You need him to give you the address of Wu Sing in Kuala Lumpur. You need it before five o'clock today.

**2**
Your name is Sam Field. You want to leave a message for Mireille Blanc. You want her to call the manager of CMJ International in France by the end of the week to discuss their new catalogue.


## 7   Messages 2 (Lesson B)                    page 31

**You are going to give two messages to Student A and take two messages from Student A.**

Don't clarify the details in your messages until A asks you to.

When A thinks they have got the messages right, they will give the same messages to you, but they will clarify all the details.

You must check that A gives you exactly the same message that you gave before.

**1**
Your name is Charlie Raven. You want to leave a message for Maureen Leigh. You need her to have 900 euros in cash ready for you by Wednesday lunchtime. (You are leaving for France and Germany on Thursday, the day after tomorrow.) You want her to tell you when you can collect the money.

**2**
Your name is Alex Petty. You want to leave a message for Vijay Iqbal. You think that he sent you the wrong attachment with the e-mail he sent at 17.05 yesterday (Tuesday). The attachment was labelled JUN FIGS and contained sales figures for June. You need the sales figures for July. This is now very urgent.

## 8    Consolidation Plus (Units 5–7)    page 33

**Answer the phone.**

Student A wants to speak to someone in Marketing who you've never heard of.

Tell A you don't know anyone of that name. Offer to put A through to someone else in Marketing.

Tell A that Vince West definitely does not work in Marketing. Start to get angry.

## 10  Appointments and arrangements (Lesson B) page 41

**You are going to receive two calls from Student A and make one call to Student A.**

**1**

You are Mr Klein's PA. Student A calls you. Accept A's apology and check the day and time of the appointment.  Offer a new appointment. Say goodbye.

**2**

Invent a name or use your own. Call Ms Teser's secretary to change the time of your appointment. Apologise. Agree to the new time offered and say thank you.

**3**

You are Lindsay Castle. You have a meeing on Tuesday at 3:00 with your colleague Stevie Fleet. Stevie calls you. Answer Stevie's questions about it. Acknowledge Stevie's thanks and say goodbye.

## 11  Recorded information (Lesson A)    page 43

**Prepare to read the information below as clearly as you can to Student A. Pay attention to stress and chunking.**

When you are ready, take turns to read your information. A should note down the important information, using abbreviations if possible.

*We are now closed until Monday January 3rd at 9 am. We will then be open every day from 9 am to 9 pm. In an emergency, please call 07862 340 904.*

## 11  Recorded information (Lesson B)    page 45

**Student A will call you and ask for information. Answer their questions using the following information. Give spellings where you think it is necessary/helpful.**

**1**

You work for Rising Sun Travel. Flights leave Tokyo for Sydney at the following times on Saturdays and take eight and a half hours: mornings – 6.50, 10.20; afternoons – 2.40, 5.30; evenings – 9.00.

**2**
You are Pat. The name of the new member of staff is Sheelagh Witherspoon and her extension number is 2556.

**Now call Student A. Make notes during these calls and check that you have written the information you're given correctly.**

**3**
Phone the Managing Director's secretary, Sam, and ask:
• what time tomorrow's meeting is
• how long it will last
• who's giving the presentation.

**4**
Ring your client Lesley and ask how to get to their office from the station.

# 12 Messages 3 (Lesson A)                    page 47

**Read the instructions below quickly and think briefly about what you are going to say. When you are ready, take turns to practise leaving messages on an answering machine / voice mail.**

When Student A gives you a cue like 'You've reached the voice mail of X. Please leave your message', give your message.

When A is giving a message, note down the important points.

Check your notes and messages together when you have finished.

**1**
Invent a name or use your own. You have an interview with the company you have called, at 11.30 this morning, but unfortunately you are sick. Apologise and ask them to call you back. Leave your name and number.

**2**
Invent a name or use your own. Call your boss's PA and leave a message saying you need to see your boss this week if possible. Leave your name and extension number and say when she can call you back.

**3**
Invent a name, company and e-mail address, or use your own or one that you know. Leave your e-mail address and ask them to e-mail the information you wanted as soon as possible.

## 12 Messages 3 (Lesson B)

page 49

**You are going to receive two calls from Student A and make two calls to Student A.**

**1**

You are Hans. Respond to Alex's call.

**2**

You are Fiona. Respond to John's call.

**3**

You are Bill. Call Tamara and tell her you can talk about the project this afternoon. Fix a time and place.

**4**

You are Juan. Phone Michel and tell him you are currently expecting 257 delegates at the conference, but there may be more – you will keep him informed.

## 13 Consolidation Plus (Units 9–12)

page 51

**You are going to make one call to Student A and receive one call from Student A.**

**1**

Invent a name or use your own. Phone Ms Lo's PA. Try to make an appointment with Ms Lo. You can't manage any of the times offered. You get angry.

**2**

You are Mr Prada's PA. Student A calls you. Offer A several appointment times. Remain calm and polite.

## 14 Telephone conferences (Lesson B)

page 55

## Participant 2

**Your name is Marta Mazo. You work for CIS as the Head of Human Resources in Brasilia. Your opinion is as follows:**

*The best option*

- staff to English-speaking countries

*Advantages*

- motivating
- offers staff travel as well as English language training

Notes

# Communication activities

## 14 Telephone conferences (Lesson B)   page 55

### Participant 3

**Your name is Mehmed Hasan. You work for CIS as Associate Director of the Bahrain office. Your opinion is as follows:**

*The best option*

- employ an in-company teacher in each branch

*Advantages*

- courses specially designed to meet staff's needs
- flexible timetable to fit in with work

*Disadvantages*

- expensive
- can interfere with work

Notes

# Communication activities

## STUDENT D

### 14 Telephone conferences (Lesson B) page 55

#### Participant 4

**Your name is Boris Grass and you are Director of Personnel at the Berlin branch of CIS. Your opinion is as follows:**

*The best option*

- give everyone the choice of how they want to learn
- give them each a certain amount to spend each year

*Advantages*

- more adult approach
- people learn better if they have a choice

*Disadvantages*

- some people may find it hard to choose

Notes

# Communication activities

## 14 Telephone conferences (Lesson B) page 55
### Participant 5

**Your name is Beata Vilic. You are Manager of the Warsaw branch of CIS.
Your opinion is as follows:**

*The best option*

- a mixture of self-study for all staff and sending key staff to an
  English-speaking country

*Advantages*

- some people need English more than others
- cost-effective

*Disadvantages*

- may cause bad feelings

Notes

# 1  Answering the phone

## Answering

Hello.
Good morning/afternoon.
Maria Roberts.
Maria speaking.
Maria here.
Extension 3557.
ABC Pizzas.
Production Department.
Can I help you?
(an answering machine message)

Call me on …
Try my mobile: …

## Phone numbers

- Use single numbers.
- Group numbers with pauses.
- *0* is pronounced 'oh' or 'zero'.
- Double numbers (like 55) are pronounced 'five-five' or 'double-five'.

## 2   Beginning a call

### Introducing yourself

This is Maria.
It's Maria here.
Maria here.
My name's Maria Roberts.

### Responding

Oh, hello, Maria / Ms Roberts.

### Asking for someone

Is that Jack Smith?
Is Jack there?
Is Jack in?

Could I speak to Jack, please?
I'd like to speak to Jack, please.

### Responding

Yes, it is. / No, it isn't.
Speaking.
No, I'm sorry, he's/she's away
this week.

Yes, of course.

### Asking someone to wait

Just a moment, please.

### Checking who is calling

I'm sorry, who shall I say is calling?
Sorry, who's calling, please?
Sorry, what did you say your name was?
And your name again?

### Clarifying who you are

It's Maria – from the New York office.
I'm a colleague of Jack's.
He's/she's my line manager.
We met at a conference last month.
He/she rang me yesterday.

### Saying why you're calling

I'm phoning/calling/ringing to discuss the conference.
I'm phoning/calling/ringing about the delivery.

## 3 Ending a call

### Signalling the end of a call

Speak/Talk to you next week.
Good to talk to you.
Glad you were in.
Nice to make contact at last.
Thank you for calling.
Thanks for calling back.
Thank you for getting back to me.
Give him my regards.
Give my regards to Jack.
Give me a ring.
Send me an e-mail.
See you soon.
Have a good weekend.
I must get on.

### Making offers

I'll send you the information in an e-mail.
I'll call again tomorrow.

### Making requests

Could you post it to me?
Could you wait till next week?

# 4   Consolidation Plus (Units 1–3)

## Saying you've got the wrong number

I'm sorry. I think I've got the wrong number.

## Responding

Don't worry.
That's OK.
No problem.

## Saying the caller has got the wrong number

I think you've got the wrong number.
This is 316549.

## Responding

Oh, sorry to trouble you.

# 5  Connecting people

## Asking for a person and a department

Could you put me through to Accounts, please?
I'd like to speak to Jack in Marketing, please.
Can I have someone in Sales, please?
Could I have the IT Department?

## Asking the caller to wait

Just a moment, please.
Hold the line, please.
Could you hold, please?
Trying to connect you.

## Telling the caller they'll be connected

Putting you through.
You're through now.
Jack can take your call now.
It's ringing for you.
OK, you're through.

## Saying someone is not available

Sorry, the line's busy at the moment.
His/her line's engaged, I'm afraid.
Would you like to hold?
I'm afraid Jack's busy just now.
He'll/she'll call you back in five minutes.
Shall I try someone else for you?

Can someone else help?

## Responding

Yes, I'll hold on.

Yes, please. Is David there?
Yes, Carol might know. Could you try her?
No, it's OK. I'll ring back after lunch.

# 6   Messages 1

## Answering someone else's phone

Jack Smith's desk.
Jack Smith's office.
Jack Smith's phone.
Jack Smith's number.
Jack Smith's extension.
Extension 482.

## Offering to take a message

Can I take a message?
Shall I take a message?
I'll take a message if you like.
Would you like me to take a message (for Jack)?
Would you like to leave a message?

## Asking for time to prepare

Just a moment while I get a pen.
Just hang on a moment then.
I'll find a notepad. Hold on.
Hold on, please. I'll get a notepad.
Can you hold on while I find a piece of paper?
Could you wait a minute then?

# 7   Messages 2

## Clarifying details when leaving a message

That's N for November.
16, that's one six.
Smith, that's spelt S-M-I-T-H.

## Checking details in messages

Sorry, what was that?
Was that A for Amsterdam?
How do you spell the name of the town?
Could you say that again more slowly, please?
Could you repeat that, please?

# 8   Consolidation Plus (Units 5–7)

## When you don't know the person the caller is asking for

I'm sorry, but I don't know anyone of that name.
I'm afraid you've made a mistake. There's no one of that name here.

## If there's no department of that name

I'm afraid we don't have a … Department. Would you like to speak
to …?

## If you think you have made a mistake

I'm sorry. I've made a mistake.
Sorry, I'll check the name and number.

# 9   Communication problems

## Responding to problems

I'm sorry, but I can't understand what you're saying.
I still don't understand, I'm afraid.
Can you speak up, please? I can't hear you very well.
I still can't hear properly. I think we've got a bad line.
Would you mind repeating that, please?
No, I still don't know what you mean.
Could you speak more slowly, please?
I'm sorry, but that's still too fast for me.
Sorry, I didn't catch that.
No, sorry, you're still breaking up.

## Dealing with problems

Is there anyone in your office who speaks Italian?
I'll call you back.
I'll try again later.
I think I'll call back when these workmen have finished.
Shall I try again when we get to the next station?
Could you ring me and see if we get a better line?
I'll send a fax with a diagram of the plan.
I'll send you an e-mail with all the details.
I know – why don't I send you an e-mail?
I'll spell it out slowly for you.
I'll ask my boss to phone you in the morning.

## 10 Appointments and arrangements

### Making appointments and arrangements

Could I make an appointment to see …?
I need to make an appointment with …
I think we need a meeting.

How about tomorrow?
What about Thursday?

May I ask what it's about?
Can you tell me what it's about?

### Confirming times and days

Yes, that's fine. Friday, 2.30.
So that's Thursday 29th at 9.30.

### Checking details

I just wanted to check the time of our meeting.
Was it 1.15 or 1.30?

### Changing and cancelling appointments and arrangements

I have to cancel the appointment.
Would you like to make another appointment?
Could we make it a different day?
What about Wednesday instead?

# 11 Recorded information

## Understanding recorded information

If you have a star button, please press it now.
For trains to Brussels, please press 1.
If you are unsure of which option to choose, please hold and you will be connected to one of our operators.
You are now held in a queue and your call will be answered as soon as possible.
In an emergency, call …

## Asking for information

Could I have some information about …?
I'd like some information about …
I'd like to speak to someone about …
I'm enquiring about …
I'd like to ask about …
Could you tell me a bit more about …?
Could you tell me how to …?

## Giving information

OK … the address is …
Right, the number you wanted is …
We are open from nine to eight every day.

## Checking you have understood

Could you repeat that, please?
Could I just check I've got that right?
Was that 14 or 40?

## 12 Messages 3

### Understanding recorded messages

Leave your message or send a fax after the tone.
Please leave your name and address, spelling out any difficult words.
I'm sorry there's no one here to take your call.
If you'd like to leave your name and number, someone will get back to you as soon as possible.

### Leaving a message on an answering machine / voice mail

226372, that's double 2 6372.
That's S for Sugar.
Call me on …
This is a message for …
It's quite urgent.

### Responding to messages

Thanks for your message (about ...)
Thanks for calling me back.
Thanks for phoning back.
Thanks for getting back to me.
I'm just returning his call.
I've just got your message (about ...)
I've just got your e-mail (about ...)
I've just got your fax.

### Using abbreviations

| | |
|---|---|
| Mon | Monday |
| am | morning |
| dept | department |
| poss | possible |

**Try to develop your own system!**

## 13 Consolidation Plus (Units 9–12)

### When you can't reach agreement

I'm sorry. I think we'll have to leave it for now.
It seems it's just not possible at the moment.
Let's try again in a few days/weeks.

### Responding

That's OK.
That's all right.

## 14 Telephone conferences

### Presenting information

I'm A and I'm chairing the meeting.
I've organised this meeting to discuss the English language
training project.
I work in Human Resources.

### Expressing an opinion

Well, personally, I think the best solution is …
Well, in my opinion, …
I feel that generally …
I really think it would be better to …

### Agreeing

I certainly agree.
I completely agree with you.
That sounds like a very good idea to me.

### Disagreeing

I'm not sure I agree with that.
I don't agree that …

# 1 Answering the phone

## Lesson A

**1.1**

1 Hello.
2 Good morning. Jo Cobb speaking.
3 ABC Pizzas.
4 Sorry I'm not here to answer your call. Call me on 01273 56218, or try my mobile: 07977 8142015.
5 Maria Roberts.
6 Production Department. Can I help you?
7 Extension 3557.
8 CUP Publishing. Piero Dolce here.

**1.2**

1 Hello. Can I help you?
2 Maria Roberts speaking.
3 RMG. Tom here.
4 Extension 0248.
5 Good afternoon.
6 SQC International.
7 Please call me on 890375.
8 Sales Department. Anna here.
9 Extension 517. Hello.
10 Good morning. BTG Telephones.

**1.3**

1 Hello.
2 Good morning. Jo Cobb speaking.
3 Sorry I'm not here to answer your call. Call me on 01273 56218, or try my mobile: 07977 8142015.
4 Maria Roberts.
5 Extension 3557.
6 CUP Publishing. Piero Dolce here.
7 Hello. Can I help you?

8 Maria Roberts speaking.
9 Extension 0248.
10 Please call me on 890375.
11 Sales Department. Anna here.
12 Good morning. BTG Telephones.

**1.4**

a 677 622
b 50 24
c 439 751
d 381 1675
e 00 44 2083 165 249

**1.5**

a 078 901
b 07657 355 648
c 33 12
d 56 22 14
e 329 0847

## Lesson B

**1.6**

1 MBM. Good afternoon.
2 Hello. EAK.
3 PJB.
4 SJY. Bob Flowers.
5 TDW. Good morning.
6 ARP.

**1.7**

1 Good morning. JHA Travel.
2 GVR Engineering. Judy Evans.
3 NEQ Technology. Can I help you?
4 BIF Transport.
5 LDC Communications. Can I help you?
6 Hello. OZ Electronics.

**1.8**
A H J K
B C D E G P T V Z (AmE)
F L M N S X Z (BrE)
I Y
O
Q U W
R

# 2  Beginning a call

## Lesson A

**2.1**
**1**
A: Good morning. ABC Software.
B: This is David. Is Chris there?
A: Yes, just a moment …

**2**
A: 451. Hello.
B: It's Tina here. Could I speak to Jo, please?
A: Yes, of course …

**3**
A: Tara Travel. Good afternoon.
B: Oh, good afternoon. My name's Jana Corte. I'd like to speak to Alain, please.
A: Just a moment, please …

**4**
A: Extension 7813.
B: Miguel here. Is that Diane?
A: No, it isn't. Just a moment …

## Lesson B

**2.2**
**1**
A: Good morning. ABC Software.
B: This is David. Is Chris there?
A: Yes, just a moment … I'm sorry, who shall I say is calling?
B: David, David Banks – we met at a conference last month.

**2**
A: 451. Hello.
B: It's Tina here. Could I speak to Jo, please?
A: Yes, of course. And your name again …?
B: It's Tina – from the Sydney office.

**3**
A: Tara Travel. Good afternoon.
B: Oh, good afternoon. My name's Jana Corte. I'd like to speak to Alain, please.
A: Just a moment, please … Sorry, what did you say your name was?
B: Jana Corte – I'm a colleague of Alain's.

**4**
A: Extension 7813.
B: Miguel here. Is that Diane?
A: No, it isn't. Just a moment … Sorry, who's calling, please?
B: It's Miguel Filol – I'm phoning to check on the new design.

**2.3**
1  I'm calling about the meeting.
2  I'm ringing to ask about the next delivery.
3  It's Ana here, from head office.
4  I worked with her last month.
5  He came to a meeting at our office recently.

# 3  Ending a call

## Lesson A

**3.1**
**1**
A: So, there won't be a problem with it.
B: Yes, good. Glad you were in. I was quite worried about everything.
A: Well, thank you for phoning.
B: OK, goodbye.
A: Bye.

**2**

A: Yes, and thank you for getting back to me.

B: That's OK.

A: Oh, and give my regards to Sam, please.

B: Of course, yes, of course I will. Bye now.

A: Goodbye.

**3**

B: Did you speak to your colleague in Sales?

A: Yes, I did. Everything's fine.

B: Excellent. Well, nice to make contact at last.

A: Yes, it's been very helpful. Speak to you soon, I hope.

B: OK. Well, I'm here all next week.

A: Fine. I'll call you then. Bye for now.

B: Bye.

**4**

B: So, I think that's everything, then.

A: Yes, fine. Well, thanks for calling back.

B: No problem.

A: And let's discuss it next week.

B: Yes. Give me a ring – or send me an e-mail: rmg@lol.com.

A: rmg@lol.com. OK. Goodbye then.

B: Goodbye.

**5**

B: Anyway, good to hear about the conference.

A: Yes, it went really well.

B: OK, well, I must get on. See you soon.

A: Yes, and have a good weekend.

B: You too. Bye then.

A: Bye.

# Lesson B

**3.2**

**1**

B: So, I do need to know soon.

A: OK. And your name again …

B: Phil Davies, that's Davies with an E.

A: OK, fine. Well, thanks, Mr Davies. I'll fax the details.

B: Good. Thank you. Bye.

A: Goodbye.

**2**

A: So, I should know by then.

B: So, could you call on Tuesday?

A: Yeah, OK, I'll be back then.

B: Have a good holiday.

A: Thanks. I will. Bye then.

B: Bye-bye.

**3**

B: And it was difficult not to laugh.

A: I'm not surprised. Look, sorry, I must go.

B: Oh, right.

A: I've got a meeting in five minutes.

B: All right then. I'll deliver the package at 11 o'clock.

A: Yes, right, that'll be fine.

B: All right. Bye then.

A: See you.

**4**

B: Oh, yes, sorry, let me see … sorry …

A: That's all right.

B: Yes, here we are … it's 229 8265.

A: Sorry, could you repeat the second part?

B: Yes, it's 8265.

A: Lovely. OK, speak to you again soon.

B: Yes. Bye then.

A: Bye.

**3.3**

**1**

OK, fine. Well, thanks, Mr Davies. I'll fax the details.

**2**

So, could you call on Tuesday?

**3**

All right then. I'll deliver the package at 11 o'clock.

**4**

Sorry, could you repeat the second part?

# 4  Consolidation Plus (Units 1–3)

**4.1**

a  GVH Software.

b  07631 824975.

c  BKJ Travel.

d  2119.

# 5  Connecting people

## Lesson A

**5.1**

**1**

A: ABC Construction. Hello.

B: Hello, Tom Burns speaking. Could you put me through to Accounts, please?

A: Yes, of course. Just a moment, please … Putting you through.

**2**

A: Good morning. ABC.

B: Good morning. It's Oscar here. I'd like to speak to Todd in Marketing, please.

A: Yes. Hold the line, please. Sorry, what did you say your name was?

B: It's Oscar – from Media Plus.

A: Thank you … Todd can take your call now.

**3**

A: ABC. Tracy here. How can I help you?

B: Can I have someone in IT, please?

A: And your name is …?

B: Susi. Susi Lo.

A: OK, Ms Lo … You're through now.

**4**

A: ABC.

B: Hello, this is Peter. Could I have the Personnel Department?

A: Sorry, which department do you want?

B: Personnel … Human Resources, please.

A: Human Resources. Right, could you hold, please? … It's ringing for you.

## Lesson B

**5.2**

**1**

A: ABC. Good morning.

B: Oh, good morning. Could I have the Marketing Department?

A: Yes, hold on, please … Sorry, the line's busy at the moment. Would you like to hold?

B: Yes, I'll hold on.

A: Thank you …

**2**

A: ABC Construction.

B: Could you put me through to Lynn in Customer Services?

A: Customer Services. Right, I'll try to connect you … I'm afraid Lynn is busy just now. Shall I try someone else for you?

B: Oh, no, it's OK, I'll ring back after lunch.

**3**

A: Hello, this is ABC.

B: Hello, this is Owen. Could I have Accounts, please?

A: Just a moment, please … It's ringing for you.

B: Thanks …

C: Jean in Accounts. Can I help you?

**4**

A: ABC Construction. How can I help you?

B: I'd like to speak to Hans in Personnel.

A: Fine. And you are …?

B: Jaroslav Novotný.

A: Hold the line, please, Mr Novotný … OK, you're through.

C: Hans speaking.

**5**

A: Good afternoon. ABC.

B: Could I speak to Sue, please, in the IT Department?

A: Of course. Who's calling, please?

B: Amanda Bell.

A: Trying to connect you … Ms Bell, she'll call you back in five minutes. Is that OK?

B: Yes, that's fine, but I'll be out after two.

**6**

A: ABC. Tracy speaking.

B: Hi, this is Steve of Jameson and Co. Can I have Gordon in Sales, please?

A: Gordon, yes, hold on … His line's engaged, I'm afraid. Can someone else help?

B: Yes, Elena might know. Could you try her?

**5.3**

**1**

A: ABC. Good morning.

B: Oh, good morning. Could I have the Marketing Department?

A: Yes, hold on, please … Sorry, the line's busy at the moment. Would you like to hold?

B: Yes, I'll hold on.

A: Thank you …

**2**

A: ABC Construction.

B: Could you put me through to Lynn in Customer Services?

A: Customer Services. Right, I'll try to connect you … I'm afraid Lynn is busy just now. Shall I try someone else for you?

B: Oh, no, it's OK, I'll ring back after lunch.

**3**

A: Good afternoon. ABC.

B: Could I speak to Sue, please, in the IT Department?

A: Of course. Who's calling, please?

B: Amanda Bell.

A: Trying to connect you … Ms Bell, she'll call you back in five minutes. Is that OK?

B: Yes, that's fine, but I'll be out after two.

**4**

A: ABC. Tracy speaking.

B: Hi, this is Steve of Jameson and Co. Can I have Gordon in Sales, please?

A: Gordon, yes, hold on … His line's engaged, I'm afraid. Can someone else help?

B: Yes, Elena might know. Could you try her?

**5.4**

Sorry, the line's busy at the moment.

His line's engaged, I'm afraid.

I'm afraid Lynn is busy just now.

She'll call you back in five minutes.

**5.5**

A: Would you like to hold?

B: Yes, I will for a couple of minutes.

A: Shall I try someone else for you?

B: Yes, please. Is Anna there?

A: Could you call back later?

B: Yes, I'll ring back this afternoon.

# 6 Messages 1

## Lesson A

### 6.1

**1**

A: Clare Aston's desk.

B: Hello, is Clare there, please?

A: No, I'm afraid she's on holiday this week.

B: Oh, is she?

A: Yes. Can I take a message?

B: Yes, that would be very kind of you.

A: OK, just a moment while I get a pen …

**2**

A: Ole Kirsten's office.

B: Hello, can I speak to Ole, please?

A: No, I'm sorry. He's in a meeting at the moment.

B: Oh, dear …

A: Would you like to leave a message?

B: Oh, yes, thanks.

A: Just hang on a moment then …

**3**

A: Terry and Co. Sam Shilton's phone.

B: Hello, this is Jean Cork of First Solutions. Is Mr Shilton available?

A: Sorry, but he's away from his desk just now.

B: Oh, no, this is really urgent.

A: I'll take a message if you like.

B: Could you? Thanks.

A: No problem. I'll find a notepad. Hold on …

## Lesson B

### 6.2

**1**

OK, so this is Mike Turner from the Manchester office. Could she e-mail her report to me by Thursday, please?

**2**

I've got some questions about the conference in July. I need him to phone me as soon as possible. And my name's Khan, that's K-H-A-N.

**3**

Yes, so it's Fernando de los Rios of West One Studios. Just to confirm I'll be coming on Tuesday, that's the 14th. I'll be there at 2 o'clock.

**4**

I'm from EQ Electrics – Tricia Smart. I haven't received the package yet. Can she call me about it? The number's 01242 679824. Or she can e-mail me. My address is t.smart@eqelec.com.

### 6.3

**1**

A: Would you like me to take a message for Jan, Ms Rivers?

B: Oh, thanks.

A: Just a moment then … OK …

B: Right, well, she rang me last week about a delivery for next month. I wonder if she's got the details yet. Could she fax them or e-mail them to me if she has?

A: OK, I'll give her the message when I see her …

**2**

A: Would you like to leave a message?

B: Yes. Could you tell Melis that Sara phoned? Could she phone me back? Next week would be fine but not Tuesday as I'm off then.

A: Fine, I'll tell her …

**3**

A: Can I take a message?

B: Yes, tell Jo that Ken would like him to fax the order before 12 tomorrow, no, Thursday. Then I can make sure the new machines arrive at the beginning of May.

A: The beginning of May. Fine. I'll see that he gets that …

**4**

A: You can leave a message if you want.

B: Yes, that would be good.

A: I'll just get a pen … Right.

B: OK, well, this isn't really urgent but if Nita could phone tomorrow, we can plan the agenda for next month's meeting. And my name's Jose.

A: Right, Jose, I'll make sure that she gets the message.

**6.4**

**1**

It's Cathy – I can't come to the meeting on Tuesday. Can we change it to Wednesday?

**2**

This is Alex – Ella is arriving at 3.30 tomorrow. Could you meet her at the station?

**6.5**

**1**

A: I'm afraid Pete's in a meeting.

B: Oh, not again!

A: Yes … Shall I take a message?

B: Yes, please.

A: Could you wait a minute then?

B: OK.

A: Right, what's the message?

B: The new designs are ready now but I need to discuss them with him – we need to check some figures.

A: And your name again?

B: Chris, Chris Archer of Supersports. And my number is 222 4018.

A: All right. I'll leave that on his desk …

**2**

A: Oh, well, don't worry.

B: It's OK, I'll take a message for Martha if you like … but can you hold on while I find a piece of paper?

A: Yes, fine …

B: OK then, Ms Jones.

A: Right, I really need her monthly report today. If she can't e-mail it through before four, could she phone me and explain what the problem is?

B: OK. I'll let her know as soon as she comes in …

# 7 Messages 2

## Lesson A

**7.1**

**1**

And he needs to speak to Nicole on 00 31 (for France) 22 58 90 66.

**2**

Tell her I'll finish typing the report and send it to SITA Software when she's checked it.

**3**

Please could he send 16 new motors to me at the Derby warehouse?

**4**

I'd like him to e-mail me at pgreen@mac.com next week before I go to Hamburg.

**5**

She needs to contact the manager of the Sales Department and tell him the final total is 35,850.

**7.2**

**1**

And he needs to speak to Nicole, that's N for November-I-C-O-L-E, on 00 31 (for France) 22 58 90 66. That's oh oh three one two two five eight nine zero six six.

**2**

Tell her I'll finish typing the report and send it to SITA Software – that's S for Sugar-I-T for Tom-A – when she's checked it.

**3**

Please could he send 16, that's one six, new motors to me at the Derby warehouse? The Derby warehouse. Derby is spelt D for David-E-R-B for Brother-Y for Yellow.

**4**

I'd like him to e-mail me at pgreen@mac.com – that's all lower case, no capitals, P for Peter, Green at M for Music, A, C dot com – next week before I go to Hamburg, that's Hamburg, South Africa.

**5**

She needs to contact the manager of the Sales Department and tell him the final total is 35,850, that's three five eight five zero.

## Lesson B

**7.3**

**1**

I've just got the flight details. We need to check in at five o'clock in the morning. And the flight number is HA6 401.

**2**

OK, then, it's 70, Old Street, and that's in a town called Reading.

**3**

Right, well, he wanted to know about the new model 39573X, which will be ready in March. And it's going to cost $59.50, that's from the beginning of March.

**7.4**

**1**

A: … Yes, OK then.
B: I've just got the flight details. We need to check in at five o'clock in the morning.
A: Sorry, what was that – the check-in time?
B: Five o'clock in the morning.
A: OK.
B: And the flight number is HA6 401.

A: Was that A for Amsterdam, J for John?
B: No, H for Henry, A for Amsterdam.
A: Oh, right. HA.
B: Yes …

**2**

A: … OK, just a moment, please. Right.
B: OK, then, it's 70, Old Street …
A: Sorry, was that 17 or 70?
B: 70, seven oh. 70, Old Street, and that's in a town called Reading.
A: 70, Old Street. OK. And how do you spell the name of the town?
B: It's Reading, that's R-E for Edward-A-D for Dog-I for Ice cream-N for Nothing-G.
A: R-E-A-D-I-N-G.
B: That's it, so I hope to …

**3**

A: … Yes, of course. OK.
B: Right, well, he wanted to know about the new model 39573X, which will be ready in March.
A: Sorry, but could you say the model number again more slowly?
B: 39573X. OK?
A: Yes, thanks.
B: And it's going to cost $59.50, that's from the beginning of March.
A: Could you repeat that, please – the price?
B: Yes, 59, that's five nine dollars and 50, five oh, cents.
A: $59.50, right, from the beginning of March …

**7.5**

1 How do you spell that?
2 Could you repeat that, please?
3 Sorry, but could you say that again more slowly?
4 Sorry, what was that?
5 Sorry, was that 17 or 70?
6 Was that A for Amsterdam or H for Harry?

## 8 Consolidation Plus (Units 5–7)

### 8.1
**1**
A: Good morning. Micro World.
B: Good morning. Could you put me through to Pierre White in IT, please?
A: I'm afraid he's not in today. Can I take a message?
B: Yes, please. Could you tell him Joe Brandt called, that's Joe with an E, Brandt, B-R-A-N-D-T.
A: Mm hmm.
B: I need him to fax me some info about the conference.
A: OK, I'll tell him.
B: Thanks.

**2**
A: Hello, CC Solutions.
B: Oh, hello. Could I speak to Maria in Customer Services, please?
A: Just a moment … She's busy right now. Would you like to leave a message?
B: Yes, please. This is Pauline Richards from travelwithus.com. Could you ask her to ring me back as soon as possible?
A: Does she have your number?
B: Yes, she does.
A: OK.

**3**
A: … well, it is rather urgent.
B: Shall I take a message?
A: Yeah, if you wouldn't mind.
B: Hold on while I get a pen … OK.
A: Could you tell her Jack phoned? I'm afraid I can't make the meeting this afternoon.
B: Yes, don't worry. I'll make sure she gets the message.
A: Thank you.

### 8.2
… yes, it's Silvia from the Rio office. I need to speak to Frank urgently to check the time of his flight. Can he tell me if he's arriving at 2.30 in the morning or the afternoon on October 26th?

## 9 Communication problems

### Lesson A

#### 9.1
**1**
A: … so I hope that you'll be able to join me and my colleagues for lunch at Al Forno's after the meeting. At about 1.30, I should think.
B: I'm sorry, but I can't understand what you're saying.
A: Oh, right, well, we're having lunch at Al Forno's after the meeting. At about 1.30. Would you like to come?
B: I still don't understand, I'm afraid.

**2**
A: … and I know that she's busy all morning on the 6th, I'm afraid. After lunch is probably OK. Can I make the appointment for 2.15?
B: Can you speak up, please? I can't hear you very well.
A: Oh, OK, yes, sorry. She can't see you in the morning on the 6th. What about 2.15 in the afternoon?
B: I still can't hear properly. I think we've got a bad line.

**3**
A: … and after that you find the small switch located just to the left of the main on/off switch. Press it once and then everything will be fine.
B: Would you mind repeating that, please?
A: There's a small switch – it's just to the left of the on/off switch. Find that and then press it once.
B: No, I still don't know what you mean.

**4**

A: I'd like you to send it to me at 70A, West 34th Street, San Diego, CA – and the zip code is 98102.

B: Could you speak more slowly, please?

A: Yes, of course. The address is 70A, West 34th Street, San Diego, CA 98102, right?

B: I'm sorry, but that's still too fast for me.

**5**

A: OK, so the train's getting in at half past four, and then …

B: Sorry, you're breaking up.

A: Half past four, and then the bus leaves at ten to five.

B: No, sorry, you're still breaking up.

**9.2**

**1**

OK, so my new address is Halco House, Charlton Industrial Estate, Woolwich, London SE18 5EZ.

**2**

OK, so my new address is 53 Regency Drive, Tunbridge Wells, Kent, TN24 7JY.

**3**

OK, so my new address is Reading Towers, Grovelands Business Park, Bracknell, Berkshire, RG35 9BW.

## Lesson B

**9.3**

**1**

A: Oh, right, well, we're having lunch at Al Forno's after the meeting. At about 1.30. Would you like to come?

B: I still don't understand, I'm afraid.

A: Oh, dear. Well, is there anyone in your office who speaks Italian?

B: Oh, yes, there is. Hold on a moment …

**2**

A: Oh, OK, yes, sorry. She can't see you in the morning on the 6th. What about 2.15 in the afternoon?

B: I still can't hear properly. I think we've got a bad line.

A: Yes, it's not very good, is it? OK, I'll call you back.

B: Fine, speak to you later.

**3**

A: There's a small switch – it's just to the left of the on/off switch. Find that and then press it once.

B: No, I still don't know what you mean.

A: All right, then. I'll send you an e-mail with all the details.

B: Oh, good idea. Thank you very much.

**4**

A: Yes, of course. The address is 70A, West 34th Street, San Diego, CA 98102, right?

B: I'm sorry, but that's still too fast for me.

A: I'll spell it out slowly for you. OK?

B: Yes, that should be fine.

**5**

A: Half past four, and then the bus leaves at ten to five.

B: No, sorry, you're still breaking up.

A: And now we're going into a tunnel … Look, I'm going to ring off now and try again later.

B: OK, speak to you soon, then.

**9.4**

**1**

A: I'll send a fax with all the information.

B: OK, good idea.

**2**

A: I know – why don't I send you an e-mail?

B: Thanks very much.

**3**

A: Is there anyone else I could talk to?

B: Yes ... hold on a moment.

**4**

A: I'll ask my boss to phone you in the morning.

B: That would be helpful. Thanks.

**5**

A: Could you ring me and see if we get a better line?

B: Yes, of course I will.

# 10 Appointments and arrangements

## Lesson A

**10.1**

**1**

A: Hello. Tom Pink's desk.

B: Oh, hello, Tom. It's Susan here. How's the project going?

A: Not bad, but I think we need a meeting soon to discuss it.

B: OK. How about lunchtime tomorrow?

A: Yes, fine. Let's meet in the canteen at 1.15.

B: OK, fine. See you then.

**2**

A: Good morning. ISI Bank.

B: Could I speak to Mr Fischer, please?

A: He's in a meeting at the moment. Can I help?

B: It's Imran Shah here. Could I make an appointment to see him sometime this week?

A: Just a moment. I'll check his diary ... What about Friday 14th at 2.30?

B: Yes, that's fine. Friday, 2.30.

A: May I ask what it's about?

B: I'd like to talk to him about some new investments.

A: OK, fine. We'll see you then.

B: Thanks very much.

A: You're welcome. Goodbye.

B: Bye.

**3**

A: Good afternoon. Ray Cohen's office.

B: Hello. This is Kumiko Chen from Accounts. I need to make an appointment with Mr Cohen as soon as possible.

A: Just one second, Ms Chen ... When would suit you?

B: In the morning if possible ... This Wednesday or Thursday?

A: What about Thursday at 9.30?

B: That's perfect.

A: Can you tell me what it's about?

B: Yes, it's about the latest sales figures.

A: All right, I'll put it in his diary ... So that's Thursday 29th at 9.30.

B: Thank you very much.

A: Don't mention it. Goodbye.

B: Goodbye.

## Lesson B

**10.2**

**1**

A: Oh, hello, is that Susan?

B: Speaking.

A: Hello, Susan, Tom here. I just wanted to check the time of our meeting tomorrow. Was it 1.15 or 1.30?

B: It was 1.15 – in the canteen.

A: OK. Sorry about that.

B: That's OK. Bye.

**2**

A: Good morning. Can I help you?

B: Oh, yes, please. It's Imran Shah here. I made an appointment to see Mr Fischer on Friday.

A: Yes, I remember.

B: I do apologise, but I have to cancel it.

A: It's quite all right. Don't worry about it. Would you like to make another appointment?

B: No, I'll just cancel it for now.

A: OK, Mr Shah, that's fine. Goodbye.

B: Goodbye.

**3**

A: Ray Cohen's office. Can I help you?

B: Well, I hope so. I have an appointment with Mr Cohen next Thursday – the 29th – at 9.30.

A: Yes … Ms Chen?

B: Yes, that's right. I'm really sorry, but could we make it a different day?

A: That's all right. Just a moment … What about Wednesday instead?

B: Wednesday 28th?

A: Yes, Wednesday 28th at 11.30.

B: That's great. Thank you very much.

A: Not at all. Goodbye.

B: Goodbye.

**10.3**

I just wanted to check the time of our meeting tomorrow.

Was it 1.15 or 1.30?

I have to cancel it.

Would you like to make another appointment?

Could we make it a different day?

What about Wednesday instead?

# 11 Recorded information

## Lesson A

**11.1**

Welcome to the Office Equipment information line. If you have a star button, please press it now. Thank you. You now have three choices. For general enquiries, please press 1. For information on this month's special offers, press 2. For information on delivery times, press 3. This month's special offers. For further details, please press 4 for office furniture, press 5 for stationery supplies and 6 for computers. Computers menu. To find out more about notebook computers, please press 7. To find out about desktop computers, press 8. If you are unsure of which option to choose, please hold and you will be connected to one of our operators as soon as possible …

**11.2**

**1**

Hello. This is updated information on Fast Trains' timetable for tomorrow June 7th up to midday. For trains from Amsterdam to Brussels, press 1. For trains … Amsterdam to Brussels. There are trains every hour on the hour from 6 am, plus extra trains on the half hour at 6.30, 7.30 and 8.30 am. Journey time is approximately 3 hours 40 minutes.

**2**

Hello. You've reached Message Plus, the smart way to process your calls and receive your messages. This month we have some really special offers. If you sign up and pay in the next five days, you can receive a whole month's message processing totally free of charge and two months at the very special discounted price of £33.95 per month. You will also be automatically entered for our prize draw with the chance to win £1,000 worth of computer equipment.

**3**

Hello. You're through to TBT. We are now closed until Monday, February 10th and will then be open from 8 am to 8 pm Monday to Saturday and 9 am to 4 pm Sunday. In an emergency, call 08000 276 523.

## Lesson B

**11.3**

If you are unsure of which option to choose, please hold and you will be connected to one of our operators as soon as possible … Thank you for calling the Office Equipment information line. You are now held in a queue and your call will be answered as soon as possible …

A: Hello, OE Information line, Deirdre speaking. How may I help you?

B: Yes, good morning. I'd like some information about notebook computers, please.

A: Yes. Do you have our catalogue in front of you?

B: Yes, I do. I'd like to ask about model C76035.

A: Go ahead.

B: It says it's on special offer this month.

A: Just let me check for you ... C76035 ... yes, indeed, there's a very good discount of £100 – only until the end of October, though.

B: So, how much is it then?

A: One moment ... that's £1,195 + VAT at £208, making a total of, er, £1,403.

B: Is that before or after the discount?

A: That's with the discount. The normal price is £1,295, excluding VAT.

B: Could I just check I've got that right? That's a total of £1,403, but just during October.

A: That's correct.

B: OK, I think I'll get back to you.

A: Fine. Just ask for Deirdre.

B: I will. Thanks very much.

A: You're welcome. Goodbye.

B: Bye.

### 11.4

**1**

A: Good morning. DCA.

B: Oh, hello. I'm enquiring about your advertisement in *The Post*.

A: Yes, go ahead.

B: Could you tell me a bit more about your offers on mobile phones?

A: Well, you really need to phone the information hotline – that's 07976 15358.

B: Was that 1-5 or 1-9?

A: 15358.

B: So, that's 07976 15358. Are they open now?

A: Yes, it's a 24-hour information service.

B: OK, thanks very much.

A: Don't mention it. Bye.

B: Goodbye.

**2**

A: Good afternoon. CCB.

B: Good afternoon. I'd like to speak to someone about the conference.

A: Well, I can probably help.

B: OK. Could you tell me how to get there from the station, please?

A: Yes, of course. Come out of the station, cross over the main road, turn left and take the first right. That's South Cross Way. The conference building is number 17 – 17, South Cross Way.

B: Could you just repeat the address, please?

A: Yes, sure. It's 17, that's 1-7, South Cross Way.

B: All right. Thanks a lot.

A: No problem. Goodbye.

B: Bye.

### 11.5

A: The reference number is 1457RT.

B: Was that T for Tom or D for David?

A: I'd like to speak to someone about an invoice, please.

B: I'll put you through to Accounts.

A: Could you just repeat the number, please?

B: Yes, it's 09763 425713.

A: I'd like some more information about the programme, please.

B: Well, I can probably help.

A: Was that Tuesday or Thursday?

B: It's Thursday 26th.

# 12 Messages 3

## Lesson A

### 12.1
**1**

This is 0245 777 836. Leave a message or send a fax after the tone.

**2**

Hello. This is Next Day special delivery line. Please leave your name and address, spelling out any difficult words, and we will send the catalogue to you as soon as possible.

**3**

Hello. I'm sorry there's no one here to take your call, but if you'd like to leave your name and number, someone will get back to you as soon as possible.

**4**

The office is now closed. Our office hours are 9 to 5.30 Monday to Friday. Please call again during those times or visit our website at www.comprint.com.

**5**

I'm not here this afternoon. You can get me on my mobile – 07998 637461.

**6**

Hello. You're through to our direct Infoline. If you want Technical Services, please press 1. For Accounts, press 2. To speak to one of our Customer Advisers, please press 3.

### 12.2
**1**

This is Stephan Freund, that's Stephan with PH, wanting to speak to Ms Sanchez. Call me on 0783 double 2 6372, that's 0783 22 6372, or e-mail me. The address is s.freund@jkint.com, that's S dot FREUND, F-R-E-U-N-D, at jkint dot com. It's quite urgent. Thank you.

**2**

Yes. My name's Ali Rashid, that's Ali – A-L-I, Rashid – that's R-A-S for Sugar-H-I-D, address 3A, 3 A for Apple, 18, 1-8, Broadway, all one word, Stockton, S-T-O-C-K-T-O-N, TN 23 6EZ.

**3**

This is a message for Mr Corradini from Sara Yorke. I'd like to change my appointment with him from Tuesday morning to Thursday morning at the same time, if possible. I think he has my number, but it's 0203 665992.

## Lesson B

### 12.3
**1**

A: Oh, hi, John. It's Sue.

B: Hello, Sue.

A: I've just got your e-mail – about changing the meeting to Tuesday. That's fine.

B: Oh good.

A: OK. See you then.

B: Thanks for getting back to me. Bye.

**2**

Hello. This is a message for Santi from Corinna. I'm just returning his call. I'm catching the 8.32 Eurostar to Paris on Friday, arriving at half past twelve local time. I hope that's OK. Let me know if there's a problem. Bye.

**3**

A: Bella Richardson.

B: Hello, Bella. It's Bob. Thanks for your message.

A: That's OK.

B: Can you schedule me for three interviews on Wednesday afternoon, between two and five?

A: Yes, that's fine. Thanks for calling me back.

B: No problem. Bye.

### 12.4

Thanks for calling me back.

Thanks for your message.

I've just got your message.

I'm just returning his call.

Thanks for phoning back.

I've just got your e-mail.

I've just got your fax.

Thanks for getting back to me.

## 13 Consolidation Plus (Units 9–12)

**13.1**

A: GTSB Bank. Good morning.

B: Oh, hello. I'd like some information about investments.

A: Well, you really need to speak to one of our financial advisers. Would you like me to make an appointment?

B: Oh, OK ... er ... yes, please.

A: Let me see ... with Mr Schmidt? When would suit you?

B: What about next week sometime?

A: I'll just check his diary ... How about Tuesday afternoon at 2.30?

B: Could you repeat that, please? It's rather a bad line.

A: Certainly. Tuesday at 2.30.

B: Could I just check I've got that right? Tuesday 19th at 2.30 with Mr ... Schulz?

A: No, with Mr Schmidt.

B: Oh, I'm terribly sorry.

A: That's quite all right.

B: Could you spell that, please?

A: Yes, it's S-C-H-M-I-D-T.

B: S-C-H-M-I-D-T. OK, thanks very much. Goodbye.

A: You're welcome. Goodbye.

## 14 Telephone conferences

## Lesson A

**14.1**

MICHEL: Hello, hello. Is everybody there? This is Paris calling. I ...

ALL: I'm here. Hello. Sorry? Who's speaking, please? Hello.

GLEN: Hang on a minute, shouldn't we ...?

SUSI: I don't think this is going to work really ... Look, I'm in Beijing and ...

LOLA: Well, I'm in Mexico City and I really can't hear anyone very well.

GLEN: I can hear all right but it's midnight here. I'm in Seoul and I'm really not sure whose idea this conference was, but ...

IVAN: Could I just say something, please? I haven't had a chance yet. I'm in Moscow and I'm really not sure what this meeting is about. Is it ...?

**14.2**

MICHEL: Well, hello, everyone. I hope we're all present. I'll just introduce myself first and then perhaps we can each do the same in this order – Glen in Seoul, Susi in Beijing, Lola in Mexico City and then Ivan in Moscow. OK, I'm Michel Lefevre and I'm chairing this meeting. I am the Managing Director at the Paris office and, as you know, I've organised this meeting to discuss the English language training project. Right ... Glen. Glen?

GLEN: Yes, hello. My name's Glen Parsons, and I work in Human Resources at the Seoul office.

MICHEL: Susi?

SUSI: Hello, everybody. I'm Susi Tan and I am the Personnel Manager of the Beijing branch.

MICHEL: Thank you. Lola? ... Lola Sanchez?

LOLA: Yes, hello. I'm the Assistant Director at the offices here in Mexico City.

MICHEL: And Ivan? ... Hello, Ivan, are you there?

IVAN: Yes, hello. I'm here. My name is Ivan Karpov and I'm the Director in Moscow.

MICHEL: Good. Thank you very much everybody. Now, if ...

**14.3**

MICHEL: … Now, I hope you've all had a chance to look at the agenda and prepare to talk about what you think is the best way to spend this money. Shall we go in the same order as before and each say what we think? I think we can allow interruptions here, if it seems important.

ALL: Yes, that's OK … OK… OK.

MICHEL: Well, personally, I think the best solution is an extensive evening or lunchtime course for our more junior staff, and then also to send some of our more key staff to Australia for short, intensive courses. Glen?

GLEN: Well, I certainly agree that some staff should be sent to an English-speaking country but I'm not sure about Australia. Also, I don't agree that evening and lunchtime courses are very cost-effective. I feel that generally people aren't very motivated by them.

SUSI: I completely agree with you – I've had the experience of evening and lunchtime courses myself and they can be a problem. I really think it would be better to send everyone to an English-speaking country.

GLEN: I'm not sure I agree with that. It's far too expensive.

MICHEL: Lola and Ivan, you haven't said anything yet. Lola?

LOLA: Well, in my opinion, if we employ a teacher in each of our offices, we can make sure the teacher is competent at teaching English for specific purposes and is able to motivate our employees. I think that would probably work out more economical because of all the travel costs.

MICHEL: Ivan?

IVAN: Yes, well, I agree with you, Lola. An in-company teacher would be great. That sounds like a very good idea to me.

MICHEL: Well, shall we now have a look at each of these options in more detail …

**14.4**

I'm A and I'm chairing this meeting.
Well, personally, I think the best solution is …
I certainly agree.
I completely agree with you.
Well, in my opinion, …
I'm not sure I agree with that.
I feel that generally …
I work in Human Resources.
That sounds like a very good idea to me.
I don't agree that …
I've organised this meeting to discuss …
I really think it would be better to …

# Unit 1

## Lesson A

### Listening 1
a person's name  (2), 5, 8
a company's name  3, 8
a department name  6
an extension number  7
two phone numbers  4

### Listening 2
1 Hello    2 speaking    3 ABC
4 answer your call; Call; mobile: **07977
  8142015**    5 Maria
6 Department. Can I help you?
7 Extension 3557
8 CUP; here

### Language focus
Pronunciation:
1 The people in 3 and 6
2 Ticks: 1, 2, 4, 7, 8, 10
1 b 50|24    c 439|751    d 381|1675
  e 00|44|2083|165|249
2 a 078 901    b 07657 355 648    c 33 12
  d 56 22 14    e 329 0847

## Lesson B

### Listening 1
2 EAK    3 PJB    4 SJY    5 TDW    6 ARP

### Listening 2
2 a    3 d    4 b    5 c    6 f

### Language focus
Pronunciation:
The letters are grouped according to the
seven sounds listed in the table.

# Unit 2

## Lesson A

### Listening 1
1 ABC Software    2 451    3 (Tara) Travel
4 7813

### Listening 2
*Introducing yourself*
1 This is    2 It's; here    3 My name's
4 here
*Asking for someone*
1 there    2 Could I    3 like to speak to
4 Is that

### Language focus
1 c    2 a    3 e    4 b    5 d
Also possible: 2 c, d, e, 4 e, 5 e

## Lesson B

### Introduction
1 c    2 d    3 a    4 b    5 f    6 e

### Listening 1
Ticks:
Sorry, who's calling, please?  (4)
I'm sorry, who shall I say is calling?  (1)
Sorry, what did you say your name was? (3)
And your name again …?  (2)

### Listening 2
say why they are calling  4 (to check on
the new design)
mention something that happened
recently  1 (met at a conference last
month)
say where they're from  2 (the Sydney
office)
describe their relationship  3 (a colleague
of Alain's)

### Language focus
1 about    2 to    3 from/at
4 with/for    5 at
Pronunciation:
1 I'm calling about the meeting.
2 I'm ringing to ask about the next
  delivery.
3 It's Ana here, from head office.
4 I worked with her last month.
5 He came to a meeting at our office
  recently.
The words with important information
(often verbs and nouns) are stressed.

# Unit 3

## Lesson A

### Introduction
1 call    2 'Goodbye'    3 harder
4 person    5 finish    6 this
7 politely

### Listening 1
1 the man    2 Sam    3 the woman
4 rmg@lol.com    5 the woman

### Listening 2
2 Thank you for phoning.
3 Thank you for getting back to me.
4 Give my regards to …
5 Nice to make contact at last.
6 Speak to you soon.
7 Thanks for calling back.
8 Give me a ring or send me an e-mail.
9 Good to hear about …
10 I must get on.
*I must get on* is the most direct way of showing you want a call to end.

### Language focus
(Suggested answers)
*Infinitive (without 'to')*
Speak/Talk to you in ten minutes / this afternoon / tomorrow / on Thursday …
*Adjective + infinitive (with 'to')*
Good/Nice/Great to talk to you / get your call / hear from you …
*Imperative*
Say 'Hello' to John / Say 'Hi' to Ann / Give my regards/best wishes/love to Steve …
*Thank you / Thanks for* getting in touch / letting me know about … / returning the call so quickly …

### Practice
**1**
1 Sorry, but I really must get on now.
2 All right. Well, thanks for calling.
3 That's OK. Speak to you soon.
4 Yes, bye.
OR
1 Sorry, but I really must get on now.
2 That's OK. Speak to you soon.
3 All right. Well, thanks for calling.
4 Yes, bye.
**2**
1 Thank you for ringing.
2 That's OK. Good to speak to you again.
3 And give my regards to Bob.
4 Of course I will. See you then.
5 Yes, bye.

**3**
1 Speak to you next week then.
2 Fine. I'm away on Monday, though.
3 Oh, are you? OK.
4 Right, well, good to hear from you.
5 Yes, nice to talk to you, too.
6 Bye for now.
7 Goodbye.

## Lesson B

### Introduction
2 Give them my regards then.
3 Thank you very much for calling me back.
4 Talk to you later then.
5 Have a good weekend.
6 Nice to make contact at last.

### Listening 1
a time  3  11 o'clock
a day  2  Tuesday
a telephone number  4  229 8265

### Listening 2
1 I'll
2 could you; Tuesday?
3 deliver; I'll deliver the package at 11 o'clock.
4 repeat; second; could you repeat the second part?

### Language focus
Pronunciation:
(Brackets show where pauses are likely but not essential.)
2 So|could you call on Tuesday?
3 All right then.|I'll deliver the package (|) at 11 o'clock.
4 Sorry,|could you repeat the second part?

2 I'll e-mail the November report to you.
3 I'll call you tomorrow afternoon.
4 Could you discuss the problem with your boss?
5 Could you phone me back?
6 I'll work late so that I can finish the report.

# Unit 4

## Listening
**1** a GVH Software   b 07631 824975
c BKJ Travel   d 2119

## Language focus
1 B: Can/Could; to
  A: shall; say; calling/speaking
  B: It's
2 A: contact   B: getting
  A: I'll   B: regards
3 A: calling/phoning/ringing
  B: glad/pleased   A: Could/Can
  B: I'll          A: Speak/Talk

# Unit 5

## Lesson A

### Introduction
IT (Information Technology) – computers
etc.
Customer Services – customers' enquiries
Human Resources – staff
Marketing – advertising
Accounts – invoices, bills, salaries, etc.
Sales - selling

### Listening 1
IT  3  Human Resources  4  Marketing  2
Accounts  1

### Listening 2
1 Putting   2 Hold; line   3 Can; have
4 a Could; have   b ringing for

### Language focus
*Asking for a department/person*
1 Can I have someone in IT, please?
  Could I have the Personnel Department?
2 Could you put me through to Accounts,
  please?
  I'd like to speak to Todd in Marketing,
  please.
*Asking someone to wait*
1 Hold the line, please.
2 Just a moment, please.
  Could you hold, please?
*Connecting*
1 Putting you through.
  It's ringing for you.
2 Todd can take your call now.
  You're through now.

## Practice
**1**
1 Key Finance Company. Can I help you?
2 Oh, good morning. I'd like to speak to
  Mr Costa in IT, please.
3 Fine. Who shall I say is calling?
4 Ann Thompson.
5 Thank you. Hold the line, please … It's
  ringing for you …
**2**
1 Key Finance Company. How can I help
  you?
2 Good afternoon. Could I have someone
  in Accounts, please?
3 Accounts, yes. And your name is …?
4 Rob Sparkes. S-P-A-R-K-E-S.
5 Trying to connect you, Mr Sparkes …
  Putting you through to Accounts now …

## Lesson B

### Introduction
1 Human Resources Department
2 What did you say your name was? /
  And your name is? / Who shall I
  say is calling?
3 Hold the line, please. / Just a
  moment, please. / Could you hold,
  please?
4 Putting you through. / X can take your
  call now. / You're through now. / It's
  ringing for you.

### Listening 1
Ticks: 3, 4
Crosses: 1, 2, 5, 6

### Listening 2
**1**
already on the phone  1, 4
doing something else  2
going to phone the caller back  3
**2**
1 the line's busy   2 engaged   3 I'm
afraid; is busy   4 She'll call; back

### Language focus
1 b   2 c   3 a
Pronunciation:
The intonation rises on all the questions
(including *Is Anna there?*) and falls on the
responses.

# Unit 6

## Lesson A

### Listening 1
1 on holiday    2 in a meeting
3 away from his desk

### Listening 2
1 Aston's desk; I'm afraid; on holiday; take a message; while I get a pen
2 Kirsten's office; in a meeting; Would you like to leave; hang on
3 phone; but; away; desk; I'll take a; if you like; I'll find; Hold on

### Language focus
1
*Offering to take a message*
Can I take a message?
Would you like to leave a message?
I'll take a message if you like.
*Asking for time to prepare*
OK, just a moment while I get a pen.
Just hang on a moment then.
I'll find a notepad. Hold on.

## Lesson B

### Listening 1
2 Ms Khan; questions; July conference; Phone; soon; possible
3 Fernando de los Rios; West One Studios; coming; Tuesday 14th; 2
4 Tricia Smart; EQ Electrics; hasn't received; package; Call; 01242 679824; e-mail; t.smart@eqelec.com
The callers stress the key words.
The key words are the words with important information: usually verbs and nouns – especially names, days and times, numbers, addresses.

### Listening 2
1 last = next
2 next Tuesday = next week, but not Tuesday
3 correct
4 Urgent = Not urgent

### Language focus
(Suggested answer)
Paula from Sales rang. Please call her as soon as you get in.
Pronunciation:
1 Cathy; can't come; meeting; Tuesday; change; Wednesday

Cathy can't come to the meeting on Tuesday. Can you change it to Wednesday?
2 Alex; Ella; arriving; 3.30 tomorrow; meet; station
Alex called. Ella is arriving at 3.30 tomorrow. Can you meet her at the station?

### Practice
(Suggested answers)
1 Pete – Chris Archer of Supersports rang. The new designs are ready. He needs to discuss them with you and check some figures. His number is 222 4018.
2 Martha – Ms Jones called. She wants your monthly report today. E-mail it before 4 or phone her to explain the problem.

# Unit 7

## Lesson A
### Introduction
(Suggested answers)
Think about important details; write the message; underline important information.

### Listening 1
a request to receive something  3
the name of a department  5
a place where the caller is going  4
a telephone number  1
an offer to finish something  2

### Listening 2
1 00 31 22 58 90 66; Nicole
2 finish typing and send the report; SITA Software
3 16 new motors; Derby
4 Hamburg (South Africa); pgreen@mac.com
5 Sales Department; 35,850

### Language focus
1
| | |
|---|---|
| S for Sugar | F |
| T for Tom | D |
| D for David | T |
| B for Brother | P |
| Y for Yellow | I |
| P for Peter | B |
| M for Music | N |

**2**
a 22 – two two
b 0 – zero
c 16 – one six
d 35,850 – three five eight five zero
**3**
(Suggested answers)
a five six double two one four / five six two two one four
b two oh two double six three four one two / two zero two six six three four one two
c seven oh seven nine double eight eight one four nine / seven oh seven nine eight double eight one four nine / seven zero seven nine eight eight eight one four nine
d four hundred and fifteen / four one five
e eighteen thousand eight hundred and eighty-eight / one eight eight eight eight
f six hundred and fourteen thousand two hundred and sixty / six one four two six oh/zero

## Lesson B

**Introduction**
2 spell    3 common    4 numbers
5 single

**Listening 1**
b 2    c 1    d 3    e 3    f 1

**Listening 2**
a R-E-A-D-I-N-G
b 70
c No, H for Henry, A for Amsterdam
d $59.50 (59 dollars and 50 cents)
e 39573X
f 5 o'clock in the morning

**Language focus**
Pronunciation:
The voice rises at the end of them except 5 and 6.

# Unit 8

**Listening**
**1** 1 b    2 b    3 b
**2** (Suggested answer)
Frank – urgent. Silvia from Rio needs to speak to you to check your flight time. Is it 2.30 am or pm on 26/10?

**Language focus**
1 Could you put me through to Jacob in Accounts, please?
2 His line's busy at the moment. Can someone else help?
3 Yes, could you try Zeta in Sales? She might know.
4 Sorry. Her line's engaged, too.
5 Oh, dear ... it is rather urgent.
6 Would you like me to take a message?
7 Oh, yes, please. That's very kind of you.
8 Just a moment while I get a pen.

# Unit 9

## Lesson A

**Introduction**
(Suggested answers)
Speaking fast; speaking quietly; bad English; technical problems.

**Listening 1**
an address  4
an appointment  2
an invitation  1
an explanation  3
travel details  5

**Listening 2**
1 a I can't understand
  b still don't understand
2 a speak up
  b still can't; properly; we've; a bad line
3 a mind repeating that
  b don't know what you mean
4 a Could you speak more slowly
  b that's still too fast
5 a you're breaking up
  b you're still breaking up

**Language focus**
(Suggested answers)
**1**
1 not explaining clearly  1, 3, 4
2 speaking with a strong accent   1, 3
3 speaking fast  1, 3, 4
4 having problems with a mobile phone  5, 2
5 not speaking loudly enough  2, 1, 3

**2**
1 You're still speaking too fast.
2 I still can't hear anything.
3 I still don't know what you mean.
4 The line is still bad.
5 I still haven't found what I'm looking for.
We put *still* **after** the verb *to be* and **before** modals and auxiliaries.

### Practice
**1**
(Suggested answers)
1 Could you speak more slowly?
2 Would you mind repeating that?
3 Could you speak up?
*Would you mind repeating that?* and *I can't understand what you're saying* could be used for all of them.

## Lesson B

### Listening 1
offers to spell something  4
says they'll communicate in some other way  1, 3
says they will phone again  2, 5

### Listening 2
1 Is there anyone in your office who speaks Italian?
2 I'll call you back.
3 I'll send you an e-mail with all the details.
4 I'll spell it out slowly for you.
5 I'm going to ring off now and try again later.

### Language focus
1 b, c and e are possible
2 b, c and e are possible
3 a    4 b, c and e are possible
5 c and d are possible
Pronunciation:
(Brackets show where pauses are likely but not essential.)
1 I'll send a fax | with all the information.
  OK, | good idea.
2 I know | – why don't I send you an e-mail?
  Thanks very much. [can't be divided]
3 Is there anyone else (|) I could talk to?
  Yes | ... hold on a moment.
4 I'll ask my boss (|) to phone you in the morning.
  That would be helpful. | Thanks.
5 Could you ring me | and see if we get a better line?
  Yes, | of course I will.

# Unit 10

## Lesson A

### Introduction
appointment: boss, accountant, bank manager
arrangement: friend, husband/wife, business partner
either: colleague

### Listening 1
secretary and client  2
boss's PA and employee  3
colleagues  1

In conversation 1 they are making an arrangement; in 2 and 3 an appointment.

### Listening 2
**1**
need a meeting; to discuss
How about
Let's meet
**2**
make an appointment; see
check; diary. What about
that's fine
it's about

### Language focus
*To say you want to meet/see someone*
I think we need a meeting …
Let's meet …
Could I make an appointment to see …?
3 I need to make an appointment with …
*To suggest a time and day*
How about …?
What about …?
*To confirm a time and day*
Yes/OK, fine.
Yes, that's fine.
3 That's perfect.
*To ask about the subject of the meeting*
May I ask what it's about?
3 Can you tell me what it's about?

## Lesson B

**Introduction**
1 c    2 d    3 e    4 b    5 f    6 h    7 a
8 g

**Listening 1**
1 confirm    2 cancel    3 change

**Listening 2**
**1**
1 I just wanted to check the time of our meeting tomorrow. Was it 1.15 or 1.30?
2 It was 1.15 – in the canteen.
3 OK. Sorry about that.
4 That's OK. Bye.
**2**
1 I made an appointment to see Mr Fischer on Friday.
2 Yes, I remember.
3 I do apologise, but I have to cancel it.
4 It's quite all right. Don't worry about it. Would you like to make another appointment?
5 No, I'll just cancel it for now.
**3**
1 I have an appointment with Mr Cohen next Thursday – the 29th – at 9.30.
2 Yes … Ms Chen?
3 Yes, that's right. I'm really sorry, but could we make it a different day?
4 That's all right. Just a moment … What about Wednesday instead?
5 Wednesday 28th?
6 Yes, Wednesday 28th at 11.30.
7 That's great. Thank you very much.

**Language focus**
*Checking*
I just wanted to check the time of our meeting tomorrow. Was it 1.15 or 1.30?
*Changing*
I have to cancel it.
Would you like to make another appointment?
Could we make it a different day?
What about Wednesday instead?

Pronunciation:
I just wanted to <u>check</u> the <u>time</u> of our <u>meeting</u> <u>tomorrow</u>.
Was it 1.<u>15</u> or 1.<u>30</u>?
I have to <u>cancel</u> it.
Would you like to make <u>another</u> <u>appointment</u>?
Could we <u>make</u> it a <u>different day</u>?
What about <u>Wednesday</u> instead?

# Unit 11

## Lesson A

**Listening 1**
hash/square key – bottom right
star key – bottom left
1) star    2) 2    3) 6    4) 7

**Listening 2**
**1**
1 b    2 b    3 a
**2**
1 Train info – Amsterdam to Brussels. Every hr on the hr from **6** am + **6.30, 7.30, 8.30**. Journey time **3** hrs 40 mins (approx).
2 Message Plus – pay next **5** days, receive **a month** free + 2 mths @£33.95 per mth. Prize draw – £1,000 worth of computer equipment.
3 **TBT** – closed till Mon Feb **10th** then open Mon to Sat 8 am to **8** pm + Sun **9** am to 4 pm. In emergency, call 08000 276 **5**23

**Language focus**
**1**
info – information          mth(s) – month(s)
hr(s) – hour(s)             @ – at
am – in the morning        Mon – Monday
mins – minutes             Feb – February
approx – approximately     Sat – Saturday
wks – weeks                pm – in the afternoon

**2**
(Suggested answers)
1 Tim is arriving next week – on Tuesday at about 10 o'clock in the morning.
2 Office opening hours are Monday to Friday from 8 in the morning to 6 in the evening, and Saturday from 9 in the morning to 1 in the afternoon.
3 Price information: for six weeks only, laptop computers at/cost £995 or C1,495.

## Lesson B

### Introduction
2 G   3 C   4 G   5 A   6 A   7 C   8 C
9 A   10 G

### Listening 1
Model: C76035
Special price (without VAT): £1,195
VAT: £208
Total: £1,403
Offer valid until: 31 October / the end of
October

### Listening 2
**1**
1 (offers on) mobile phones
2 (directions to) a conference
**2**
1
I'm enquiring about
a bit more about
Was that
So, that's
2
speak to someone about the conference
can probably
Could you tell me how
Could you just repeat

### Language focus
1 c   2 a  (e is also possible)   3 d   4 e
5 b
Pronunciation: The intonation falls at the
end of all of them except 2, 3 and e.

# Unit 12

## Lesson A

### Listening 1
1 Leave a message or send a fax.
2 Leave your name and address.
3 Leave your name and number.
4 Phone again or contact a website.
5 Call a different number.
6 Press a button on your keypad.

### Listening 2
**1**
The information is clarified in
messages 1 and 2.
**2**
1 that's Stephan with PH; that's 078322
  6372; that's S dot Freund, F-R-E-U-N-D
2 that's R-A-S for Sugar-H-I-D; 3 A
  for Apple; one eight; all one word;
  S-T-O-C-K-T-O-N

### Language focus
(Repeating the whole number:) that's 0783
226372
Spelling the whole word: S-T-O-C-K-T-O-N
Using words to clarify letters: A for Apple,
S for Sugar
Repeating the number in a different way:
double 2 = 22; 18 = one eight
Saying something is one word, not two:
Broadway, all one word

## Lesson B

### Introduction
Do you want to talk? Call now.
Call me this afternoon before 6.
Are you busy tonight? How about
meeting?

### Listening 1
someone wanting to arrange some
interviews  3
someone confirming travel
arrangements  2
someone agreeing to change the day of a
meeting  1

### Listening 2
Ticks:
Thanks for calling me back.
Thanks for your message.
I'm just returning his call.
I've just got your e-mail.
Thanks for getting back to me.

**Language focus**
**1**
Thanks for your message
Thanks for calling me back / phoning back
/ getting back to me
I've just got your message / e-mail / fax
(= a short time ago)
I'm just returning his call  (= only)
**2**
1 asap – as soon as possible
  re – about/regarding    Tues – Tuesday
  am – morning
2 appt – appointment    Mon – Monday
  Fri – Friday    poss – possible
3 pm – afternoon    dept – department
4 conf – conference    nos – numbers

## Unit 13

**Listening**
1 b    2 a    3 c    4 a    5 b

**Language focus**
1 like; make; appointment; see
2 about
3 May/Could/Can; about
4 Could/Can; check; right

## Unit 14

## Lesson A

**Introduction**
(Suggested answers)
1 Participants can be anywhere in the
  world; they save time and money.
2 Finding a suitable time; not seeing other
  people's faces; talking on the phone to
  more than one person.

New York 7 am    São Paulo 9 am
Tokyo 9 pm    Seoul 9 pm
Warsaw 1 pm

**Listening 1**
**1**
Ticks: Mexico City, Moscow, Seoul, Paris,
Beijing

**2**
It wasn't clear who was speaking.
One person (in Mexico) couldn't hear very
well.
It was midnight for one person (in Seoul).
One person (in Moscow) didn't know what
the meeting was about.
The phone conference wasn't properly
planned or organised.
**3**
Seoul midnight (=GMT 3 pm)
Paris 4 pm    Beijing 11 pm
Mexico City 9 am    Moscow 6 pm
A better time to have the conference
would be 10 pm in Seoul (=GMT 1 pm) so
it would be 2 pm in Paris, 9 pm in Beijing,
7 am in Mexico City and 4 pm in Moscow.

**Listening 2**
**1**
Michel Lefevre: Managing Director, Paris
Glen Parsons: Human Resources, Seoul
Susi Tan: Personnel Manager, Beijing
Lola Sanchez: Assistant Director, Mexico
City
Ivan Karpov: Director, Moscow
**2**
Michel Lefevre: lunchtime/evening
courses; send staff to an English-
speaking country
Glen Parsons: lunchtime/evening
courses; send staff to an English-
speaking country
Susi Tan: lunchtime/evening courses;
send staff to an English-speaking country
Lola Sanchez: employ an in-company
teacher
Ivan Karpov: employ an in-company
teacher
**Language focus**
**1**
1 c    2 d    3 e    4 f    5 b    6 a
**2**
1 P    2 O    3 A    4 A    5 O    6 D
7 O    8 P    9 A    10 D    11 P    12 O/D

# Unit 15

**1**
Cross: 3
**2**
(Suggested answers)
Could/Can I speak to …?
Is … there/in?
I'd like to speak to …, please.
**3**
1 regards   2 calling   3 Have
4 Speak
**4**
1 c   2 e   3 b   4 a   5 d
**5**
(Suggested answers)
Would you like to leave a message?
Shall/Can I take a message?
Would you like me to take a message?
I'll take a message if you like.
**6**
(Suggested answers)
check – the details/the time/the
day/the date/the information/the
spelling/the number
take – your name/your number/a
message/down the details
give – someone a ring/someone a
message/me some more information
send – an e-mail/a fax/the details
make – a phone call/an
appointment/an arrangement
**7**
1  Could I speak to Jan in IT, please?
2  Thanks for getting back to me.
3  I am just returning his call.
4  I still don't understand what you are
   saying.
5  Would you like to leave a message?
6  I need to see her as soon as possible.

**8**
(Suggested answers)
1 Could you <u>fax</u> the <u>details</u> <u>today</u>?
2 The <u>boss</u> needs to <u>cancel</u> the <u>meeting</u>
  on <u>Tuesday</u>.
3 <u>Klara</u> wants to <u>change</u> her
  <u>appointment</u> to a <u>later</u> <u>date</u>.
4 I need some <u>information</u> about the
  <u>sales conference</u>.
5 Could you <u>contact Pedro before 5</u> this
  <u>afternoon</u>?
**9**
1 as soon as possible
2 regarding/about
3 conference
4 possible
5 number
6 appointment
7 department
8 morning
**10**
 1 Good morning. Could I speak to Jack
   in Marketing, please?
 2 Certainly. I'll put you through.
 3 Jack here.
 4 Oh, hello, Jack. It's Ken.
 5 Hello, Ken … er, sorry. Can you speak
   up? I can't hear you.
 6 Is that any better?
 7 No. I still can't hear you properly.
 8 I think we've got a bad line then.
   Shall I call you again?
 9 Oh, yes. Thanks very much.
10 That's OK.

# Acknowledgements

With special thanks to our parents, who did so much to develop our interest in language.

We would like to thank the following people at CUP: Will Capel for commissioning the project, Sally Searby for overseeing it from start to finish and Chris Capper for his thorough editorial work and helpful suggestions.

Thanks also to all those who gave feedback in the early stages, and to Jo Barker of Hart McLeod (design) and James Richardson (audio production).

**The publisher would like to thank the following for permission to reproduce cartoons and logos.**
CartoonBank pages 23, 31, 35, 40
CartoonStock pages 6, 10, 16, 20, 45, 47, 55
Volkswagen, His Master's Voice, British Broadcasting Corporation, BMW, DHL Worldwide Express, Cambridge University Press page 9

*Photographs*: Reeve Photography pages 6, 10, 14, 20, 24, 28, 34, 38, 42, 46, 52